TEACHING AND LE

SPELLING

Mike Torbe

PRACTICAL GUIDE SERIES

TEACHING AND LEARNING

SPELLING

Mike Torbe

Ward Lock Educational Co. Ltd.

WARD LOCK EDUCATIONAL CO. LTD.
BIC LING KEE HOUSE
1 CHRISTOPHER ROAD
EAST GRINSTEAD
SUSSEX RH19 3BT
UNITED KINGDOM

A MEMBER OF THE LING KEE GROUP
HONG KONG • SINGAPORE • LONDON • NEW YORK

First published 1977
Second edition 1978
Reprinted 1979, 1981 (twice), 1982, 1983, 1984, 1985, 1988, 1990
Third edition 1995
Reprinted 2000
ISBN 0 7062 5217 9

Acknowledgement
The Publisher wishes to thank the Mary Evans Picture Library for the
photographs on pp 65, 81, 82

Artwork is by Syd Lewis

Printed in Hong Kong

Contents

INTRODUCTION

Some children seem to learn how to spell without much help, but most need at least some teaching. This is a manual about spelling which includes basic strategies appropriate for learners of all ages and abilities, and puts spelling in the wider context of learning to be literate.

The first step in teaching spelling is to help children to become interested in words and how they work; so it helps if you, the adult, are already interested. A concern for words and their structure is part of an attitude to spelling which is more important than rote-learning the spelling of individual words, and so this manual explains how to encourage the right attitude to spelling in your children.

It also does two other things. It shows that the way learners feel about themselves is important to their learning; and it demonstrates how to integrate the teaching of spelling into the overall teaching of literacy. Experience shows that many learners can spell correctly in tests and exercises, but not in their free writing which is, after all, where they must be able to spell if they are to be confident writers. I have found, therefore, that it is more useful to support spelling in the course of writing than to have separate spelling lessons, although lessons can be useful as part of the basic strategy, especially if they are seen as a way of learning how written language works.

Although there are a few new ideas here, much of the manual derives from the researched work on spelling over the last sixty years, and readers who are familiar with the research will recognise where many of the approaches came from. Indeed, the idea for the book grew originally out of my attempts to interpret research findings practically to help my own teaching, and then from conversations with teachers I met who said how difficult it was to find accessible advice on spelling teaching.

PREFACE TO THIRD EDITION

The fact that the original *Teaching Spelling* has sold steadily since its first publication in 1977 is an indication of how important spelling has always been. I want to repeat here what I have said to numerous students, their teachers and their parents: that although accurate spelling is socially important, someone who has difficulty with spelling is not therefore unintelligent. Throughout life, indeed, *everyone* has difficulty with spelling sometimes, and being able to spell, though important, is less important than having something to write and being able to express it in writing.

Several things have changed since I last revised this text in 1978. Few people then had access to computers, and no one could have foreseen the way the microchip would affect our day-to-day lives, including our writing. Inevitably, a book on spelling must acknowledge the impact of technology, and how keyboarding, word-processing and spell-checkers have changed our approach to writing, in the same way that calculators have changed our view of basic mathematics.

What has not changed is the continuing debate about standards and accuracy, or the political importance of spelling. There is no shortage of opinion about the rights and wrongs of the debate: there is, I think, a shortage of knowledge and information. I hope this book contributes to the knowledge, rather than adding to the opinions.

Over the years, young people, parents and teachers have spoken to me about their own or their children's spelling, and those conversations have helped me to shape the present contents of the book. I thank all those people, and hope that what they find here will be helpful to them. I acknowledge especially Eddie, then 12 years old, who said to me, "Teachers keep telling me I can't spell. I know that already. They keep saying 'You must improve your spelling', but they never tell me *how*." It is because Eddie wanted to know *how*, that this new edition is called 'Teaching *and Learning* Spelling'. To Eddie, and to all those who want to know *how*, this book is dedicated.

ACKNOWLEDGEMENTS

Standing as I am on the shoulders of giants, I would like to acknowledge publicly my debt to the major workers in the field – Arvidson, Fernald, Peters and Schonell. In addition, my thanks are due to colleagues who advised me with the original edition, especially Anne Baker, Julie Jones, Colin McCall, David Pritchard and Mike Wallerstein.

My thanks also to all those who have advised and helped me with this new edition: Helen Atwood, Margaret Buck, Kate Glavina, Ann Ketch, Hilary Minns, Phil Moore and Rob Redfern.

Finally, I thank the teachers and children in Coventry schools who provided such interesting examples of writing and spelling: Howes Primary School, Stivichall Primary School, Whitmore Park Primary School and Sidney Stringer School and Community College.

PART ONE

The first part contains practical advice to readers about what to do and how to do it. It has four chapters, each with several sections.

Chapter One: Learning to spell, and what goes wrong

Chapter Two: Self as learner, self as speller

Chapter Three: Practical teaching and organisation

Chapter Four: Analysis

Each chapter is prefaced with a summary, explaining in more detail what it contains.

Chapter One

LEARNING TO SPELL, AND WHAT GOES WRONG

1.1 *LEARNING TO SPELL describes the stages of development we go through as we learn to spell, and gives examples from the work of children, young people and adults. It suggests what you should look for in order to identify someone's stage of spelling, and also discusses those who move through the stages very slowly.*

1.2 *PROBLEMS WITH SPELLING defines the reasons for people being successful or unsuccessful spellers, and what their characteristics are.*

1.3 *WHAT GOES WRONG? focuses attention on the words themselves, and shows you how to begin categorising the kinds of miscues and errors that writers make.*

1.1 LEARNING TO SPELL

If people think they have problems with spelling, they tend to ask three questions:

❏ What's wrong with my spelling?
❏ Can I get better?
❏ What can I do about it?

One answer to the first question may be "Nothing at all: it's just the normal stage of development you're at with spelling." In that case, the answers to the other two questions are "Probably", and "Take your time, but develop good spelling habits".

But another answer may be: "You are moving through the stages of development more slowly than other people do. That doesn't mean you are stupid. You can do something about it; but you will have to sort out for yourself what works best for you."

The stages of development

As children develop as writers, they appear to go through five different stages (Gentry 1982). The stages do not neatly follow each other: learners can stay at the same stage for some time, move on, and then return later to the same stage or an earlier one.

However, in broad developmental terms, learning to spell works like this, according to Gentry.

Stage 1: Precommunicative

This earliest stage describes children who are learning about literacy in general, and beginning to understand that symbols on a page mean something. Although they are not yet ready to write properly many children, if they have the opportunity, are keen to try and communicate. Their writing may use invented symbols, representing what the child thinks of as words, but with no knowledge of how letters represent sounds, or which direction to use for letters or words. Often the 'writing' has a mixture of numbers and letters, both upper and lower case. The letters children use at this stage are often ones from their own name, especially its first letter, and there is rarely any indication of word separation.

Generally children can be at this stage when they are about 3–4, although it is their experience of books and literacy that will determine exactly when they begin to play with letters like this.

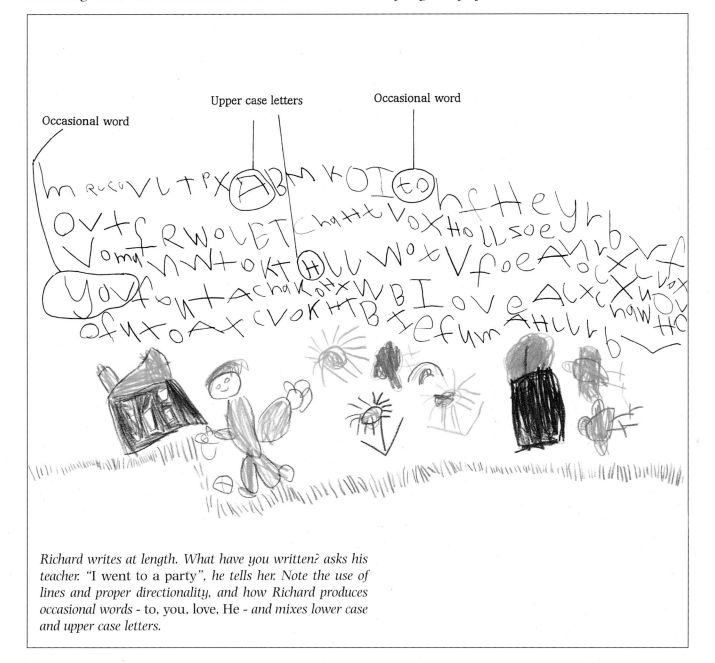

Richard writes at length. What have you written? asks his teacher. "I went to a party", he tells her. Note the use of lines and proper directionality, and how Richard produces occasional words - to, you, love, He - and mixes lower case and upper case letters.

"I am going to the park" writes Kraig (5) and uses
letters from his own name in his writing

*Alison says she has written "I am going on holiday",
and has drawn a cheerful family group ready to set off.
The words she writes are familiar ones - my, Dad, on -
but she knows enough about writing to know that you
can read it, and it tells you something.*

Stage 2: Semi-phonetic

At this stage – between the ages of 4 and 7 for most children – writers understand that letters have sounds, and begin to learn about the alphabet and letter formation. They often abbreviate words in various ways: sometimes they write only the initial letter – *d* for *dog* (5 year old); at other times they telescope the word – *cd* for *could*, for example (5 year old) – and sometimes use letter names in complex ways – *yantn* for *wire netting* (7 year old), using the letter name for *y* and the sound name for *a* to make *wire*; *drt* for *dirty*, (6 year old), using the letter name for *t* as an equivalent for *-ty*. They begin to understand directionality, though they can still reverse letters or even words.

Ryan (5) tells his teacher "I went to the park. My Dad took me". There is a clear intent to communicate, and Dad *is written twice. This writing is an example of the earliest move from the Pre-communicative to Semi-phonetic stage. Notice how Ryan signs his name to his story.*

I WatOn thetalWSo haiLOYeqMJnv

John (5) writes, "I watched a story on television". His writing is directional, but does not observe word-spacing. His letter formation is fairly accurate, and the writing begins intelligibly and then drifts into unrelated letter strings.

The pieces here show the gradual move from the pre-communicative stage towards the phonetic.

Rachel (5) writes "My Mam got a new job". She writes one word for every word in the message; the initial letters are always accurate; her attempts to spell 'new job' contain the right number of letters. Is the first word a reversal, or simply a familiar word?

'My special place is Spain because it has sand.'

Jamie is 6, writing about his 'special place'. He copies the title successfully, but most of his attempts demonstrate a random approach to spelling. Note especially his attempts to spell it has.

Alison (5) writes "Flowers have lovely petals and Pip loves flowers and Pip loves the petals." Her inventions are consistent – see famnws *for flowers, although she creates two different inventions for petals –* pucles *and* pysts. *Notice how she seems to have inserted a small T in* pucls, *and used the letter again in her second invention. She is on the point of moving into the next stage of development.*

Stage 3: Phonetic

At this stage, spelling tends to mirror sound, and writers often try and sound out everything they spell, but may not follow the patterns of English spelling. Writing is easier for the reader to interpret, because word spacing is observed, words and lines go generally in the right direction, and there tends to be a fairly good link between letter and sound.

This stage can cover a long period of development.

Children who become literate fairly quickly will enter this stage around the age of 5–6, but many writers show residual traces of phonetic spelling for some time. A writer who is younger than 8–9 and at this stage uses easily recognisable invented spellings – *wizud* for *wizard* (6 year old) for example. Look particularly at how children deal with new and difficult words, to see if they are beginning to follow the patterns of spelling.

> 22st June
>
> My holiday
>
> One Day then wos a Parcke
> and if weye ckros
> the rayall way trock
> On the last Day was
> a lawh to gow to the
> Beych on ar own. and
> the twins was frdy
> tuh. Sow weye tuch
> them Back and weye
> went Bach to, the
> Beych. and mayn a
> Deh.

Amy (7) wants to write. Like so many young children, she writes in caption, so to speak, with the rest of the story taken for granted.

One day there was a park, and if we cross the railway track on the last day was allowed to go to the beach on our own and the twins was frightened so we took them back and we went to the beach and made a den.

Notice –
ckros – *she puts the ck together at the beginning*
rayall way – *an elegant invention!*
friytun – *an excellent example of invented spelling following the sound.*
beych – *a consistent invention, as is weye*

ThursLay 23rd June Brett
I Lic to gow to BLak
pul and to sih my cusn

and to gow to fer
and sLip
Biy cus I can plir wif
plL and to gow to
gow home and to
pLey and wos tley
and gow to my cuns

Brett(7) writes
I like to go to Blackpool and see my cousin and to go
to see and sleep because I can play with people and
to go to go home and to play and watch telly and go
to my cousins.

*His spelling seems to work exclusively through sound
correspondence, using his own conventions to solve
problems*

Anthony

Thursday   23 rd   June

My   special   place

I   went   to   spun

we   go   for   aru   beckfast

and   some tames   we   go

for   a   sum   and   some tumes

we   go   on   the   bech

then   I   go   to   thus   Plac

we   done   thes   god   thung

we   made   PaP erPens

Anthony is 7, and his writing about his holiday in Spain is consistent, with reasonable versions of words. Note especially his invention for paper aeroplanes.

Adam is only 6, but his writing demonstrates the Phonetic stage very clearly, as he produces consistent inventions, all of them systematic and based on the sound.

19.1.94   Adam

There was a little boy he was Saylin

oh a boot there was a Sthme

it bowe the boot to a ilude

he wuct oh the ilude he looked

grnde the ilude he Saw Some tesar he went

up to the tesar he he Opuhd teSar

box there was tesar he chut the

tesar box a crkardyul Lesd hem

hq he got on a dovins back and went

to the uvar Soyd.

A House on fire

Once apon time there was a rabbit callded Thomas As his firthes. wore walling along a stere they saw a house on fire so one of Thomass freds went to call the fireregade they duball 999 then the firegins came as fast as they could by the time they got there the fire was going badle but they soon got it out and the pelolep wore reuse by laddal Thomass frinds got rewadd with a gold trfe and Thomas got a gold carrot the went to hosptlla and the doarra got the smoke out of the peolple

Chris (6) writes fluently. Most of his spellings are clearly phonetic attempts, though there are some features which show signs of an earlier stage. Look, for instance, at stere (street) fireregade (fire brigade - does Chris think his word is right?) badle (badly, with the letter name for e used instead of y). Oddest of all is pelelop and peolple for people: the second word is almost correct! Note the curious consistency of hosptlla and doarra (doctor).

Stage 4: Transitional

A writer at this stage follows the basic accepted patterns of English spelling, and has an increasing repertoire of correctly spelled words. Vowels are used in every syllable and the writer can make a good attempt to recall words and to spell new words. Strategies tend to depend on "sounding out" and so miscues are generally phonic alternatives. This stage can last for several years and sometimes extends well into adult life; spellers at this stage, therefore, can be as young as 6 or 7, or any age after that.

Alison is only 5, but her writing is clearly at a more advanced stage. Notice her invention for under the.

PiP WahtEd to Guow to the ZOO

John is on the borderline between the Phonetic and the Transitional stages, even though he is only 5. Most of his spelling is completely accurate, and his one invention seems to be a careful attempt to represent the sounds of the word go.

Babita

Babita is 6, and her spelling is in transition. Of the 42 words, only four are problematic – becoues, triying, herd(for heard) and nember, which appears to be a slip, because she spells it accurately elsewhere.

I am going to do my Best with my number storys becoues I get stuck on some of the numbers Thay are a bit tricky for me and Im triying very very herd with the numbers and I like my nember storys

Stage 5: Correct

'Correct' does *not* mean that every single word is spelled correctly. The writer at this stage has a basic knowledge of the English spelling system and word structure, such as prefixes and suffixes; can distinguish homonyms – words that sound the same but are spelled differently; and is increasingly accurate in the use of single and double consonants. He or she uses analogy: (because *see* is spelled with *ee*, for example, a 9 year old uses the *ee* sound in the word *deceit*), has a large spelling vocabulary, and continues to learn uncommon patterns and irregular spellings.

My Den

The Other day I Made a tent I got my
Dad's fishing umberbaba and Lots of Sheets
and I Put Pegs on the Sheets to hold Then
together and I Put Pillows under ther
to make it CorDerBell and I Made it
With Louise Woollaston and kieran came
Down and he went in it he loved it
We had it as like a litle caravan
I had my Bike outSide and I had a
roof of Corse and I had tennes
rakkets behind the chair and I enjoyed
it barry and Matthew came over
and the liked it To and what gave
my the idea off it Was I Looked
in the Shead and I finlly had
an Idea and That was to make a
big MaSSaViE Tent keeran Loved
it to barry and Matthew also Loved
it So We was Glad we made
it Louise Wollaston loved it
as well,

Claire, who is 10, writes fluently and with interest, and her spelling is on the borderline of being Correct. Her interesting and persuasive miscues – cofderbell for comfortable, and umberela – are constructed as representations of the sound as Claire hears it.

Monday 20th June.   Robert

P.G.L

All of us got on the coach and we arived at
the centre at about 3:30 then we were put into
caravans then we had free time before tea then
we had time to leran different things and then to bed
the next day I went canadin canowing I wet some pepole.
We played tig and water polo. We also ded head shoulders
krees and Jump. Two more things which were going to
the fruit shop and the hokey cokey. The next thing
we did was absaling and climing. Then we did the
mini os I endoyed the dumbling because I got up their
fast I think. The next day it was fun. We did Rifles
I hit the paper but not the target alot. The Assault
couse was fun but I didn't get to muddy I endoy ed
Junping in the mud. My favoratie bit was the rope swing.
It was ok. The best thing for me was the quards
I went on the doggy lead first

*Robert is 9, but his writing is an example of the Correct stage. His miscues may be
slips (leran) or phonetic attempts (canadin canowing). What happened with
favoratie, I wonder?*

Although these stages can be broadly related to children's ages, don't match them too precisely to age. In one group of children all the stages can be represented. One writer's spelling may show evidence of more than one stage of spelling development at the same time (see the example below); and when a writer is uncertain, he or she can often return to strategies associated with an earlier stage. Stage 5 is the beginning of the lifetime's development in spelling, because people go on developing as spellers throughout their lives.

Karyndeep's writing shows how several stages may be simultaneously present in a child's writing, in this case a 5-year old. "I am going to the park today" she says, when she's asked what she's written. But the actual words appear to be –

I at(t)o g(o) to the xxxxx to deh.

At first glance, the spelling is Pre-communicative, because of the letter formation. But it is more advanced than it appears, as the transliteration indicates. The mysterious word seems to have some letter reversals, and is probably pebek, *and thus closer to* park *than it looks.*

The features of the various stages which are present are-
Precommunicative – *no consistent spacing, inverted symbols*
Semi-phonetic – *correct directionality, reversals*
Phonetic – *letter-sound correspondence, attempt to spell* today

Adults may show very similar spelling patterns in their writing to the Phonetic stage, especially if they find writing awkward or are under stress. Their adult maturity makes them likely to understand sound-symbol correspondence, but their insecurity as spellers means they tend to produce phonic alternatives. Generally, though, once people pass the age of 13, the earliest stage that will show itself in their spelling is the Transitional.

Check where a learner's spelling would place them.

If they are **seven or less**, they are likely to be in one of the first three stages. Continue to help them to develop good spelling habits, but without creating anxiety in them.

Good habits at this stage are:
- ❏ wanting to write
- ❏ knowing the alphabet
- ❏ learning about directionality
- ❏ knowing that words are separated from each other
- ❏ understanding that all the sounds of spoken language have a written form.

Because the stages are developmental, young learners need to pass through them; so a 7 year old who appears to be at the Pre-communicative stage needs to receive the same kinds of experience as a 4–5 year old, but *relevant to a 7 year old.*

If they are **between seven and eleven years old**, and moving through the stages Semi-phonetic, Phonetic or Transitional, then again don't worry: continue to help them to develop good spelling habits.

Good habits at this stage, in addition to the ones outlined above, are:
- ❏ beginning to use dictionaries
- ❏ recognising spelling variations (for instance the possibilities of *ough*)
- ❏ knowing that not all spellings can be worked out from the sound
- ❏ being consistent with spellings (that is, for instance, spelling the same word in the same way)
- ❏ finding and recognising common parts of words.

If they are **nine or older**, up to about thirteen, expect them to be in the Transitional stage. The good habits to develop are –
- ❏ be aware of word families, prefixes, suffixes and so on
- ❏ be able to look up unfamiliar words in a dictionary

- ❏ be willing to proof-read work and self-check for spelling miscues.

Those who, for various reasons, move only slowly through the stages, tend to stick at the phonetic stage for much longer than other people. But because they live with the anxiety of feeling unsure about spelling for much longer, they may also use a whole range of other strategies, based on a fairly haphazard, arbitrary and inexplicit set of principles. So their spelling may appear random and mysterious. Unless they have very acute difficulties with language in general, such that they need highly specialised help, then they will ultimately benefit from following systematically the approaches outlined in the chapters that follow.

1.2 PROBLEMS WITH SPELLING

Once a learner or a teacher recognises the importance of the stages of development, they feel more ready to trust that their spelling will improve over time. But there still remains another question often asked:

Why do I keep getting these words wrong?

When people at any stage of development spell words incorrectly, there are usually two main reasons:
- ❏ weak visual recall
- ❏ weak auditory analysis

The most common reason is weak visual recall.

Good spellers
- ❏ hear a new word and have a range of ways which help them to associate the sounds with the right letters;
- ❏ can break a word into its parts and know how to write the parts down;
- ❏ probably see an image of the word inside the head, and "read it off" as they write;
- ❏ Will probably write the word down and see if it "looks right".

Weak spellers with weak visual recall aren't good at remembering how words should look. Their spelling errors will be recognisable as the intended word: *cof* for *cough*; *entad* for *entered*. Sometimes, the underlying logic is not immediately apparent – *girf* for *giraffe*. Is this the letter name for *f* being used: *gir* + '*ef*'? Or the letter name for *r*: *gi* + '*ar*' + *f*?

Weak spellers with weak auditory analysis have problems in saying which letter symbol represents which sound, and tend to make random and arbitrary guesses. Their spelling errors may be unrecognisable as the intended word: *michm* for *making*; *negys* for *needle*.

Don't assume that because a piece of writing contains some misspelled words the writer has a "spelling problem". Everyone makes mistakes sometimes, because of slips of the pen or blind spots with individual words.

Whatever the underlying cause of a learner's real or imagined difficulties, the basic approach recommended in this book applies to all learners. But it can be a help to both teacher and learner to decide which group a learner is in, especially if the problems continue.

Once you have considered what general stage of development a learner is in, follow the simple routine outlined in the flowchart below.

This simple checklist, together with detailed analysis when that is appropriate (see Analysis pp 60ff), will help you to define what kind of speller a learner is, and whether learners need specific help beyond the basic strategy.

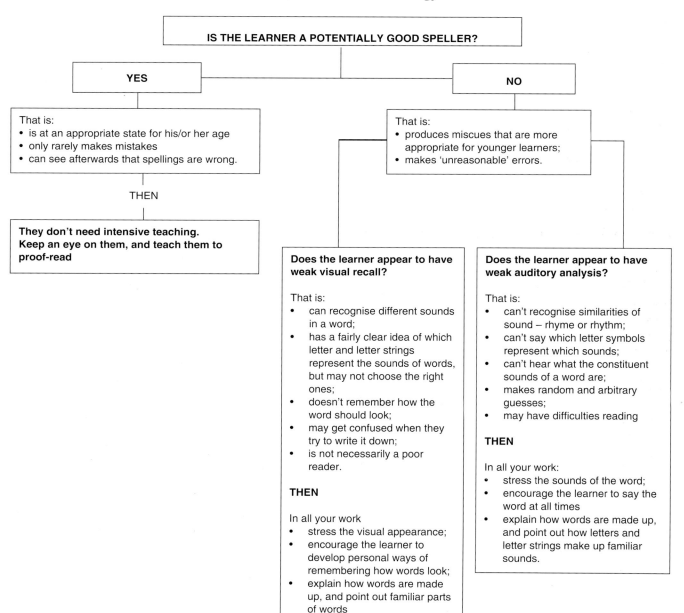

IS THE LEARNER A POTENTIALLY GOOD SPELLER?

YES

That is:
• is at an appropriate state for his/or her age
• only rarely makes mistakes
• can see afterwards that spellings are wrong.

THEN

They don't need intensive teaching. Keep an eye on them, and teach them to proof-read

NO

That is:
• produces miscues that are more appropriate for younger learners;
• makes 'unreasonable' errors.

Does the learner appear to have weak visual recall?

That is:
• can recognise different sounds in a word;
• has a fairly clear idea of which letter and letter strings represent the sounds of words, but may not choose the right ones;
• doesn't remember how the word should look;
• may get confused when they try to write it down;
• is not necessarily a poor reader.

THEN

In all your work
• stress the visual appearance;
• encourage the learner to develop personal ways of remembering how words look;
• explain how words are made up, and point out familiar parts of words

Does the learner appear to have weak auditory analysis?

That is:
• can't recognise similarities of sound – rhyme or rhythm;
• can't say which letter symbols represent which sounds;
• can't hear what the constituent sounds of a word are;
• makes random and arbitrary guesses;
• may have difficulties reading

THEN

In all your work:
• stress the sounds of the word;
• encourage the learner to say the word at all times
• explain how words are made up, and point out how letters and letter strings make up familiar sounds.

1.3 WHAT GOES WRONG?

Spelling miscues are not arbitrary and accidental. There are patterns of error for all language users: watch for them, and you can help learners more effectively. They are dealt with here in the order:

❏ initial letters
❏ phonic alternatives
❏ prefixes and suffixes
❏ unstressed syllables
❏ single/ double

*K*inds of error

1. *The initial letter* If learners make mistakes in the first consonant or initial blend, and are older than seven, they need *immediate* help with reading, and especially with phonic training.

2. *Phonic alternatives* A common error, with two main forms:

❏ The speller, not sure about the way to write a sound, chooses a pattern which is wrong here but correct in a different spelling context:
nessessary (as in *lesson*)
hows (*house*) (as in *how*)
❏ The speller may produce a form which is not possible in English spelling patterns:
au (how)
perfikt (-kt is not an English pattern; -ct is)
whrite (write)
All these errors suggest that the writer is aware of how to represent sounds, but perhaps has a weak visual memory.

◆ The first, *au* for *how*, is a vowel form that does not occur alone in English. The miscue though, is an interesting example of a 6 year old applying strict phonics (if you put your mouth ready to say *ow*, you will find that the first sound you make is *a*; move your mouth to the end of *ow*, and you will hear a sound like *oo*. The product is linguistically accurate, but not, unfortunately, accurate spelling.)

◆ *Perfikt* includes another pattern (*kt*) which is not English, probably caused by the familiar issue of *c* sounding like *k*, and the natural assumption in a young writer that therefore the sound should be written with a *k*.

◆ The third word *whrite* is perhaps more serious than the others, since *whr* is never a feature of English spelling.

When children begin to learn to write, they will *invent* spellings: that is, they use rules of their own which are logical to them, but do not follow the conventions of adult spelling. Examining the invented spellings of young children will help you to understand what they think the rules of English to be.

Some examples of invented spellings

pettule	–	**petal (5 year old)**
dowin	–	**doing (6 year old)**
sand castull	–	**sand castle (6 year old)**
pigzz	–	**pictures (6 year old)**
binocilers	–	**binoculars (6 year old)**
scalters	–	**skeletons (7 year old)**
sopostoo	–	**supposed to (9 year old)**

---

3. *Prefixes and suffixes* These cause trouble when a speller does not recognise that words can be made up of different bits brought together. Prefixes like:
dis-
in-
mis-
work by adding on to existing words, thus:
*dis*appear
*in*competent
*mis*spell

Note that *in-* changes to *im-* before words beginning with *p* or *m*:
in + material = *immaterial*
in + possible = *impossible*

Suffixes tend to cause difficulty, especially when the words to which the suffix is added end in vowels or in *l*.

-ed	*-ance*
-ly	*-ence*
-ing	*-able*
-ful	*-ible*

Everyone can be confused, because the pronunciation of the word rarely shows which suffix is the correct one. So there are very common errors, like these:

appearence	The pronunciation doesn't distinguish between *ance* and *-ence* (see 'The unstressed syllable' below).
makeing	The speller isn't certain whether the *-e* remains or goes.
lovley	The *-e* has become attracted to the *ly*, because the writer thinks of the word as a whole instead of seeing it as *love + ly*.

Help learners by drawing attention to prefixes and suffixes as separate bits of words, which are always spelled in the same way. It can also help to syllabify.

4. *The unstressed syllable* Research shows (and your own observation will confirm) that most misspellings in words of more than one syllable occur in the vowels in the unstressed syllable. There are two reasons for this.

❏ When people talk, the vowel sound in unstressed syllables almost always has the same sound as the *-er* in butter. Of all sounds in English 11% have the same *-er* noise.

❏ English uses the same vowels to represent very different sounds, but also uses different vowels to spell the same sound.

Thus:

butt*er*
pict*ure*
diff*erent* } The italicised syllables in all these words have similar sounds when
const*ant*   the words are said normally.
simil*ar*

Although the *spelling* of the final syllable is very different in the different words, the sound is more or less the same; so spellers who rely on sound rather than remembering the appearance of words can make mistakes.

Some familiar spelling difficulties are caused by the similarities in sound of unstressed syllables, the possibility of alternative spellings, and the absence of clues as to which form is preferred. Thus, for instance, the problem of *independent* or *independant*. Is there a concealed echo memory of *pendant*, when people use the incorrect form?

An associated problem is the consonant that disappears in pronunciation:

often	(generally pronounced *offen*)
Christmas	(pronounced *Chrissmas*)

Pronounce the word normally, but then point out the spelling, and offer a pronunciation that stresses the spelling: *of-ten, Christ-mas*.

5. *Single for double, double for single.* The second most common spelling miscue, after the unstressed syllable.

shining	becomes	*shinning*
dropped	becomes	*droped*

This error often produces a different word altogether, so you might expect the writer to recognise the mistake:

later	becomes	*latter*
furry	becomes	*fury*

Most readers, however, expect to read what they meant to write, and it is very easy to read an error as being correct.

Teaching should draw attention to the effect of the single or double letter combination upon the sound of the vowel; but this miscue also involves the effect of the *e*-marker.

Spelling instruction should always acknowledge the uniqueness of the learner, and do what is most helpful for that person; and so an individualised approach is always best. Remember that some things cause difficulty to everyone, however competent they are:

❏ some vowel combinations: *ie-ei* is the best known, but also *iou* and other complex combinations.

❏ unusual words using y as a vowel: *rhythm, hymn*.

❏ 'impossible' words, especially where the spelling differs markedly from pronunciation: *diphtheria, diarrhoea, eczema, fuchsia*.

If a learner is uncertain about the relationship of sound to symbol and is producing unreasonable phonic alternatives, then that must be solved before anything else is approached, by rehearsing the basic sound-symbol patterns – single letters first and then letter strings – and by focusing on visual patterns. But if you do want to devise a longer term programme, then consider the age of the learner, what stage they appear to be at, and then, when a learner's misspellings have been collected and analysed, systematic instruction can follow the order outlined above –

❏ initial letters
❏ phonic alternatives
❏ prefixes and suffixes
❏ unstressed syllables
❏ single/ double.

These five points do not cover all possible errors, but most spelling miscues fall into one or more of these groups. There is sometimes more than one reason for a miscue: always find out if an error is a real mistake that needs attention, or simply a slip of the pen that the writer may correct on re-reading.

Use the analysis-and record sheet on the next page (photocopiable) to examine a learner's spellings.

AN IMPORTANT WARNING

You will find that you will not be able to discover neat patterns in everybody's writing which make it immediately possible to categorise and cure them. Spelling – and people – are more complex than that. But the close attention you pay to the patterns will repay attention in three important ways.

1. Trying to classify them will begin to give you an insight into the causes of spelling miscues;

2. Doing it alongside the learner will show you how that individual tackles the whole problem of spelling;

3. It will show learners that the processes of spelling are not simply random, so that they can begin to help themselves to understand and control their own approach.

ANALYSIS AND RECORD SHEET

Class/child. . . . .

Date of analysis. . . . .

Initial letters	Reasonable phonic alternatives	Unreasonable phonic alternatives	Prefixes and suffixes	Unstressed syllables	Single for double/double for single

Chapter Two

SELF AS LEARNER, SELF AS SPELLER

This chapter contains four sections which recognise the importance of the learner as well as the teacher in the process of learning to spell.

2.1   *SELF-BELIEF explores the importance for learners of having a positive self-image of themselves, in order to be confident enough to learn successfully.*

2.2   *SPELLING COUNSELLING: A DEFINITION introduces the importance of counselling learners about spelling, and explains the two central ideas of spelling confidence and spelling autonomy.*

2.3   *A COUNSELLING APPROACH TO SPELLING, provides a script to follow in order to counsel learners into becoming effective learners and spellers.*

2.4   *LEARNING STYLES discusses the importance of discovering what the styles of learners are so that we can best help them, rather than impose our own styles upon them.*

2.1 SELF-BELIEF

If spellers lack trust in themselves, they *expect* that they will make mistakes when they begin writing. Watch an unconfident writer (of any age) write a word, hesitate, change it or cross it out, and produce an alternative spelling. Often the original word was spelled correctly, whereas the new one is incorrect. Why the change?

Conversations with learners persuade me that the process that goes on inside the head is like this, though it is rarely expressed as explicitly as this.

I am no good at spelling. Therefore when I spell, I will probably make a mistake.

I have written a word, but because I am a poor speller, I am frightened that it is not correct. Therefore I will change it.

I have changed it and have been told that the word is spelled incorrectly.

This proves what I feared: that I am no good at spelling. I am ashamed but resigned.

Too often, both children and adults believe that to be able to spell is a mark of intelligence and ability, and they are frightened that their spelling will show them to be unintelligent or inadequate and therefore unsuccessful. But "being able to spell" is defined publicly as being certain to spell 100% of words correctly at all times, even though that is almost certainly an impossibility. A child who consistently achieves 90% success in mathematics would be considered to be a fine mathematician; but writing and misspelling one word out of every ten would be seen as a failure.

> **Spelling is the only activity where less than 100% accuracy is considered to be failure.**

To become confident spellers, learners have to learn to trust themselves, and to believe that they are likely to spell a word correctly, rather than likely to get it wrong. Spelling confidence lies as much in the hand and the eye as in the sound and the voice. Once they gain this confidence, their self-image improves, and they become more confident writers, too. This cycle of trust and self-confidence applies to all successful learning, and one of its characteristic signs is when learners are prepared to take risks and try things out for themselves, without fearing failure.

To help learners, we must first show that we are mainly interested in what the writing says, not how it is spelled; because we must aim to help the learners build their confidence as writers. Remove the fear, and the confidence will grow.

Some case-studies

Billy is 8, and is a very dependent speller. He has become used to asking for every word he has the faintest doubt about. He writes very slowly and his handwriting is un-formed and difficult to read. With a new teacher, he expects to work in the same way, but his new teacher has a very different approach from what he has been used to. "Try it," she says; "Maybe you'll get it right. And if you're really not sure, just put the first letter and a line like this b_____"

Billy starts trying it for himself, slowly at first, with support from the teacher. "Look," she says," you've got it right," and Billy discovers that he can spell most words for himself. Those he can't, he presents as the teacher suggested. His handwriting improves dramatically, because he is now writing more rapidly and fluently, and stopping less; and his pieces of writing become longer and more complex.

Robert is 9, and his spelling concerns his mother, and, more significantly, his grandmother, who takes a great interest in his education. They try to give him help, but he gets anxious and upset and feels cheated that they should make him spend so much of his out-of-school time on spelling. His teachers notice his spelling, but beyond the usual processes of correction and class lessons do not do much about it, and certainly not enough, his family think. Because I am a family friend, they ask me to have a look at him. He reads widely and fluently, enjoys writing stories, and most of his miscues are "virtuous" – the kind that anyone could make. Most of them are about single for double letters, and about prefixes and suffixes. We talk about them, and I show him how to tackle a few of the words. I reassure the family and tell him he'll be all right. I keep in touch with Robert over the next few years. Gradually his spelling improves. When he is 13, we have a conversation about it. By now he can handle most words, and is increasingly conscious of his single-double problem. He can talk about it and explain how he tries to remember words. He has lost his anxiety, and feels confident he can handle most things.

I remark that he hadn't needed much help after all. He smiles and shrugs, and comments gently on his grandmother's tendency to get steamed up. He is pleased that as time passed, he's just naturally got better. I agree.

Michelle is 12, and very insecure with spelling. She feels vulnerable when she writes, and is worried by the big words she has to spell in her work in school subjects. She is also troubled by a range of words that she "always gets wrong". With help, she works on one or two of the words that she always has trouble with, in the way outlined in "A counselling approach". Two days after working on *necessary* she stops the teacher in the corridor and says "I can still spell it." She discovers that she can use the technique herself to study words that she finds difficult. She reports happily to her teacher that she now feels much more confident, and it doesn't worry her at first when she doesn't know a word, because she knows that she can "learn it for herself". Her spelling improves and later, in conversation, she remarks that she never has problems with spelling now, because even if she gets a word wrong, she knows she'll be able to put it right easily.

Sue is 17 and doing A-levels in Biology, Maths and Physics. She has always had difficulty with her spelling, and tends to get the right letters in the wrong order - she writes about *sexula reproduction* in Biology. The head of Post-16 education arranges for her to work intensively with a visiting advisory teacher, who discovers that Sue treats each word she can't spell as a string of letters in its own right. She does not appear to understand that the same string recurs, or that syllables, prefixes and suffixes have patterns of their own. In fact, she gets very cross with him when he explains this to her.

"Do you mean to tell me that words are made up of bits of other words?" she says angrily to him.

"Yes," he says.

"Why has no-one ever told me that before?" she demands.

Perhaps they had; but she certainly had not registered its significance. She tackles a selected list of words she knows she will have to spell in her exams, and instead of being resigned to being a "bad speller" knows now that there are regular patterns and systems. She passes her A levels, and gets the job she was hoping for as a pharmacist.

Sophie is a 25-year-old nurse. She needs to have an English qualification but consistently failed O-level English at school and afterwards, and is convinced it is because of her spelling. She begins working with me. I discover that she normally writes a word and then changes it, expecting it to be wrong. In fact, the first attempt is usually right. She explains that because she is persuaded that she is a "bad speller", she assumes that when the word she's writing is one she isn't secure about, she's got it wrong, and so automatically changes it.

After some meetings, she tells me she is going back to Jamaica to visit her family: I ask her to send me a card. She does, and then follows it up with a letter.

When she comes back, she tells me that this was the first time she has ever written a letter to anyone outside her family. We talk a good deal about how she feels about herself as a writer, and she explains how she tries to memorise the difficult words she has to write professionally, and how she has always felt insecure and "silly" when she writes.

After a few weeks of working on various things in preparation for her examination, I point out to her that in her recent writing there are no spelling errors at all. She says that she hasn't even thought about spelling as a problem, and is thinking more about what to say and how to say it. We decide that her spelling is no longer a problem to her.

2.2 SPELLING COUNSELLING: A DEFINITION

At first, many learners tend to work without much recognition of the processes they are involved in, and are not conscious of the control they can have over what they do and how they do it.

The essential idea of counselling in the context of learning is therefore:

> **To talk with individual learners before and after they do something, about their approaches, their intentions, their problems, their achievements, and how they solve problems.**

The counselling conversations help the learners to be explicit about what they do and how they do it, and therefore to be more assured.

The central concepts of spelling counselling are –
❏ spelling confidence
❏ spelling autonomy.

Spelling confidence

Break away from an excessive concentration on correctness. Learners often feel that the only reason they write is so that teachers can correct their spelling.

Learners who are not confident about their spelling become too careful, applying spelling rules to all new words with elaborate precision. They mistrust their own judgement, and often change a word properly spelled because, being "poor spellers", they do not believe that they could have got it right.

Spelling confidence means writers who are:
❏ prepared to look outside a narrow range of vocabulary
❏ primarily interested in what they are writing as an act of communication;
❏ prepared to work on public pieces of writing to check and correct spelling.

Spelling autonomy

The goal of spelling instruction is to make itself obsolete. When we can spend less time on spelling

instruction, then it has been successful.

Spelling instruction should never be seen only as an end in itself. When exercises, tests and lists feature as parts of the curriculum in their own right, then, whatever the adult claims, children come to believe that spelling matters most, rather than the authorial aspects of writing. Such a curriculum also makes the teacher central to the process, and the learners become dependent on the teacher's choice of task and its timing.

Encourage autonomy at all times. Stress the writing, so that learners recognise that every time they write they "do spelling". That is the proper time for spelling instruction – when the writer needs it, not when the teacher decides it is needed.

Spelling counselling, therefore, aims at handing the process over to the learner, not at keeping the learner dependent on the teacher. Remember:

> **The task of spelling instruction is not to correct mistakes the child has already made, but to help the writer not to make that mistake the next time.**

2.3 A COUNSELLING APPROACH TO SPELLING

This approach applies equally to children and to adults, although the way the questions are expressed may need to be adjusted for younger children. You'll need time to apply it: newcomers to the approach may be surprised how long it takes learners to make their own decisions, especially if they are unused to taking control over their own learning.

In the script and notes that follow, the questions and instructions are in bold, with an additional commentary. You may wish to keep a spelling record in which you note what the learner says, for future reference.

What do you think of your spelling?

Most people, in my experience, have a low opinion of their ability to spell, even if they are perfectly competent spellers, and are likely to answer in ways that indicate their feelings about themselves. Later, as they begin to gain confidence, you can point out their achievements and successes with some hope that they will accept and acknowledge them; but at the beginning, listen without comment to what they say.

Would you like to get better at spelling?

No one I have spoken to has ever answered "No". Without exception, learners of all ages are keen to improve, and enthusiastic about being able to spell correctly. I have never met anyone who felt that their spelling was a weakness and yet was content to leave it like that.

I can't *teach* you to be a good speller, but I can show you how to learn to spell. I'll show you what you have to do.

This is the beginning of the contract. Given the importance of learners taking responsibility for their own learning, it's important for them to realise from the outset that they will be expected to be independent. But it also establishes the important fact that you are there to support and guide rather than test and correct.

Is there a word you know you always have trouble spelling?

Most learners – but not all – will be able to choose a word which always troubles them. Sometimes the words are obvious and predictable (words such as *necessary* or *definite*) but sometimes they are unexpected and idiosyncratic. Whatever the word is, accept it. In spelling counselling, the learners must be able to trust that whatever they suggest or do will be worked with and not judged.

If they cannot recall a suitable word, look through their writing with them, and find one that they recognise they have problems with.

[You write the word down, clearly and correctly.]

It helps if you say it, once it's written, especially if the learner is one who has problems with the sounds of words.

By now you and the learner are probably sitting side-by-side, with paper between you. I shall use the word "necessary" as the example.

Which bits of the word do you have problems with?

For some learners, especially younger ones, this question will be puzzling. They may never have thought of the word as having "bits", and may not have considered the idea that their difficulty is probably not with the whole word but with some aspects of it. For this reason, and also because the process of analysing the word may be new to them, it can take some time for them to be able to indicate which parts of the word are problematic. They may indicate by pointing, or by saying it, or making the sound, or by spelling out the letters.

You may disagree with what they say, thinking that it is another part of the word that really causes the problem. That doesn't matter. It's not your word; it's their word. And their definition of the problem is what matters, even if you disagree with it.

Can you find a way of writing the word and marking it, so that you can remember the hard bit?

You may need to give examples. Here are some ways of presenting "necessary" that learners have produced.

ne - cess - ary

ne**cess**ary

ne | cessa | ry

ne<u>cess</u>ary

neCESSary

Can you say it in a way that helps you remember how it's spelled?

Again, some learners will be puzzled by this instruction; and younger children may not be able to do it at all at first. Experienced spellers often use this approach without being very aware of it as a strategy: words like *Wed-nes-day*, or *lib-rary* are often spoken or sub-vocalised by writers as reminders of how to spell them.

Now: look at the word until you're quite sure you can still see it with your eyes closed.

This is the heart of the whole approach (see *Basic Spelling Strategy p.44*). Again, it may surprise you how long it takes some learners to feel confident enough to say that they can indeed "see it with their eyes shut".

What I have observed is that learners will look at the word for a long time, and then generally shut their eyes. When they have done this a couple of times, I cover the word with my hand, and ask, "Can you still see it?" Irrespective of whether they answer Yes or No, I keep my hand there for at least 13 seconds (see *Basic Spelling Strategy*, p.44), to encourage visualisation.

Now write it down.
When they have written it down, on a fresh piece of paper, I cover what they have written and show them the original; and then cover the original and show them their own. While I do this, I ask:

Did you get it right?
Make no comment yourself on whether the word was correct or not: this process is for the learner to judge, not the teacher. Sometimes, learners will look carefully from word to word for what seems like a long time before they are prepared to say Yes or No. Whatever they say, do the same thing – reveal both words without comment, and let them do the final matching, and announce the final judgement.

If the word was spelled incorrectly, repeat the process, concentrating on the problem area revealed by the new error.

Do not move on until the learner has spelled the word correctly and feels comfortable with it.

2.4 LEARNING STYLES

Essentially, this book depends on the processes outlined in this chapter, processes by which learners become confident enough to take over the responsibility for their own spelling. When they trust themselves, they are more likely to take the risk of trying out their own idea of a word's spelling, instead of anxiously making sure it is right before they write it. And they are more likely to write freely, because they know they can go back afterwards and check on the words whose spelling they were unsure of.

Too often, spelling is associated with fear – which makes it the more satisfying and exhilarating when a learner sheds that fear and becomes able to control their writing. Part of that process is learning how one learns.

There is no one right way of learning to spell, or of teaching spelling.

Each learner will have his or her own way of tackling new learning, and of dealing with old difficulties. Their styles will probably be quite different from the teacher's learning style, too. Teachers and parents must beware of imposing their style on the learners, especially if they are much younger: adult learning patterns tend much more towards explicit rule-governed behaviour than the patterns of young people.

This is more than just casual advice: learners who feel insecure with their spelling will assume firstly

---

Basic spelling strategy

1. Write down word
2. Pronounce it clearly
3. Learner pronounce it
4. Look at word
5. Cover word up
6. Write it from memory
7. Check word
8. Re-write
9. Use word soon

vehicle

Michael   brachiosaurus

separate   Wierd

desperate   unmistakable

saleable

humorous

CONCRETE SEQUENTIAL LEARNER **Prefers a structured approach to learning** **Prefers specific schedules and requirements** **Prefers clear expectations of performance** **Values regular reviews and targets**	**ABSTRACT SEQUENTIAL LEARNER** **Works best on his or her own** **Is able to formulate theories** **Can research and learn from books** **Values one-to-one work on strategies** **and concepts**
CONCRETE GROUP LEARNER **Needs concrete experiences** **Motivated by practising spelling and** **weekly tests** **Can work with, and learn from, others**	**ABSTRACT GROUP LEARNER** **Works and learns best through** **discussion in groups** **Doesn't need fixed schedules** **Prefers open-ended assignments** **May become group leader**

(after Klein and Millar)

that teacher must know best (and will sometimes resent that); and secondly that their own style must be faulty and is certainly unsuccessful. You must support learners in discovering which style works best for them, and then in valuing and celebrating that style.

Klein and Millar (1990), who deal mainly with adult learners, present some valuable models of learning styles, as shown above, which can be usefully adapted for younger learners.

Nobody, as Klein and Millar remark, falls neatly into any one of the categories, and a learner may need a different style for different occasions: sometimes we need concrete experiences and practice, and sometimes the chance to have an open-ended discussion. But discussing the styles, especially beginning from the general invitation to learners to start by thinking about how they learn things they know they are good at, will serve many useful purposes:

❏ Learners can be assured that there is more than one way of learning;

❏ As they begin to explore their own style, learners become more confident in their general learning and transfer it to spelling;

❏ The adult-teacher, by placing his or her own learning style against these models, becomes more sensitive to the variation that is possible;

❏ The teacher can discover how best to help the learners, both as individuals and as a group.

It is worth talking to learners about what it is we

mean by learning, and what we have to learn about. Conventionally, we talk about 'knowledge, skills and understanding'. Remember that there are important differences between them, and that the kind of learning we have to do for each is different.

❏ "Knowledge" has to do with information which has been remembered and can be recalled;

❏ "Skill" has been defined as a sequence of actions which has become so routinised through practice and experience that it is performed almost automatically – and there are real questions as to whether the idea of "skill" can usefully be applied to language development and usage, because it leaves out the invention, personality and individual imagination which are fundamental aspects of language.

❏ "Understanding" is essentially the capacity to see connections between different chunks of knowledge, and to apply concepts to the solution of new challenges, not just to remember facts.

Whatever the linguistic deficiencies of spelling rules, or their intellectual difficulties, some people, especially older learners, will find them helpful and supportive because they prefer to operate in an explicitly rule-governed way. But even people who like rules will also benefit from the chance to talk things through with other learners, testing out ideas and hypotheses. A good teaching and learning style is one that is aware of alternatives, and knows that for this piece of learning, this approach is likely to be most successful; and the good teacher will make the learners aware of this, too.

Chapter Three

PRACTICAL TEACHING AND ORGANISATION

There are eight sections in this practical chapter, all designed to help you put into practice the approach and ideas of this book.

3.1   *A BASIC STRATEGY introduces some key concepts about a whole approach to teaching and learning, and describes the strategies to use with individuals, groups or a whole class. The section includes a photocopiable poster or worksheet for pupils.*

3.2   *TEACHING POINTS deals with practical advice to the teacher about helping learners.*

3.3   *DISCOVERING WHICH WORDS TO TEACH describes four approaches which will help you to begin to collect the best possible word lists to support teaching and learning.*

3.4   *ORGANISATION AT DIFFERENT LEARNING STAGES outlines some practical procedures appropriate for learners at the various stages – early (pre–5), aged 5–7, aged 7–11, aged 11–16, and as adults or young adults.*

3.5   *TEACHING IDEAS AND GAMES presents a bundle of useful ideas for teaching, including working with dictionaries, and various games.*

3.6   *The DICTIONARIES section points out the danger of taking it for granted that all learners will be able to use a dictionary, and suggests some issues to be considered.*

3.7   *This section on HANDWRITING considers this important aspect of literacy and puts it into the context of spelling.*

3.8   *The final part DOING CORRECTIONS gives practical advice about dealing with learners' writing, and includes suggestions about marking.*

3.1 A BASIC STRATEGY FOR TEACHING SPELLING

Spelling counselling is a powerful and effective approach and will be all that is necessary for some children, because it will release them from bad feelings of shame and guilt, and help them to develop their own confident approaches to spelling. But for many learners, a teacher or parent may have to do more. Just as there are different kinds of learning, so there are different approaches to teaching. Sometimes telling is important: direct instruction, to individuals, groups or the large group can be effective as long as the learners are ready for it. But at other times, learners need to share with each other, to discover and make their own rules.

What follows is an approach that you can develop as the heart of any teaching you do, whatever the style. It stresses the visual and auditory aspects of spelling, and helps learners to understand how the patterns of spelling work. It can operate for the whole class, or for individuals, and can be used whatever basic approach to teaching spelling you prefer. You will see how this fits alongside the Spelling Counselling approach advocated in Chapter 2, and how it offers learners a strategy for learning spelling.

Note here two crucial numbers: **7 ± 2**; and **13**.

7±2 represents the number of items of information that most people can hold in their short term memory at a time. It is why telephone numbers rarely exceed seven digits locally or nine long-distance, and why it is hard to recall international numbers, for instance, which can have over 11 digits, unless we rehearse them. It also explains why it is easy to forget a telephone number we have just looked up – because we only store it in our short term memory long enough to use it, and then dismiss it. Numbers we use often, on the other hand, move into our long term memory store and are easily accessible.

13 is the number of seconds something endures in short term memory before it decays, unless we do something to make it stick and shift across into long-term memory. You will see the significance of these two numbers as you look at the strategy outlined here.

The Strategy
1. Write the word down, using whatever medium you are working in (paper, word processor screen, chalk- or white-board, or overhead projector.)

2. Pronounce the word clearly and distinctly, using your normal voice, as though you are talking. If you have a regional accent, do not attempt to change it to standard English. Draw attention, if necessary, to the fact that words may not be pronounced the way their spelling suggests they will sound.

3. Ask the learner to pronounce the word in the way he or she usually does. Make sure it is pronounced distinctly. Do not correct any regional accent.

4. Give the learner time to look at the word. Draw attention to any problematic parts of the word.

If you are working with a group or a class, you will need to stress the importance of their identifying individually which part causes them difficulty, and point out that not everyone makes the same mistake with a word.

> **Encourage them to see spelling as an interesting problem to be solved, not a sin to be eradicated.**

5. When the learner is sure that they can still see the word with their eyes shut (and they should cover the word or close their eyes for at least 13 seconds) invite him or her to write the whole word from memory. They should never copy the original letter by letter. Erase or cover the original word.

6. Check the word against the original in ways that encourage the learner to remember the spelling (see *Spelling Counselling* p 39).

7. If it was right, the learner turns the paper over, or covers the first attempt, and writes it again from memory.

8. If the word was not spelled properly, repeat stages 2–5.

9. Make sure the writer uses the word again soon, but naturally, in the course of writing.

This strategy stresses the following points:
- ❑ The learner sees the word written correctly.
- ❑ An association is made between the appearance and its sound. Visual and auditory aspects are combined and can be stressed in ways that help the learning needs of individuals.

❏ Learners make their own connection between the visual and the auditory by saying the word.

❏ Learners begin to analyse and to recognise possible danger points.

❏ Visual memory is emphasised and developed.

❏ For those who learn best in auditory ways, the sounds of the word can be emphasised.

❏ The time taken helps to ensure that the word shifts into long term memory.

This strategy is for those times when you wish to give concentrated attention to spelling instruction. You can use a variant of it during normal teaching time. For example, if children ask for words while they are writing, follow the approach below. Do not write the word in the children's spelling books. Apart from meaning that children have to interrupt their writing and wait for words, it encourages them to copy without learning or understanding. Copying does not teach correct spelling. Instead:

❏ Always ask the children to have a go first, and encourage invention, so that they come to you with words already written. This will give you a clearer idea of the kinds of problem that individual children have; and anyway, they may be right!

❏ Keep a word book of your own near you – an exercise book is acceptable, but it can help to have a book with initial letters marked already, like an address book.

❏ When a child wants a word, you write it in *your* book,

❏ The learner studies it, memorises it and writes it in their own book *from memory.*

A CAUTIONARY TALE
One six year old boy, writing about dinosaurs, asked his teacher how to spell *pterodactyl.* **His teacher wrote the word in her word book, and he studied it carefully. He looked at her, back at the word, then said "You're not expecting me to remember that, are you?"**

If the same words keep reappearing (and they probably will) prepare a file-card system appropriate to the age of the learners. If you feel up to it, you can produce your own data-base or word-bank on computer for children to use, or provide a spell-checker.

Necessary conditions
The conditions necessary to help people learn to spell are that they should:

❏ See the word in print, and at the same time hear it pronounced;

❏ Fix the word in the mind before having to write it;

❏ Write it slowly enough to write it correctly;

❏ Visualise the word and "read it off" from the mental image;

❏ Write it often, and become familiar with it.

A note on time
It may appear to a teacher that putting these strategies into practice is unrealistic, given the demands of the classroom, because it will take more time than the conventional practice of writing words in the children's own spelling books.

However, consider these points:

❏ Letting the children have a go first can save time, because they may be right.

❏ Writing the words in your book provides you with a ready-made store of words which you know your pupils have difficulty with, and from which you can construct a teaching programme. In addition, if you want to choose words for a spelling test, your book provides them.

❏ Encouraging invented spellings will give the learners confidence, and help you to see how they think words are constructed.

❏ The children produce their own spelling dictionary, which is freely available to the whole class.

❏ It avoids one of the commonest problems for the primary classroom – the child who comes to the teacher for a word which is already written down higher up the page of the word book.

❏ The teacher only has to write a word once, in the teacher's word book, instead of thirty times, once in each child's book.

❏ The saving on paper is great!

Hints for the pupil
In addition to teaching children directly, you can give them their own strategy. "How to help yourself to spell", on the next page can be presented as a classroom poster, or as a stick-in sheet for exercise books. If you introduce learners to this strategy, you are *teaching them how to learn.* Point out those parts of the strategy that are most useful if someone learns

How to help yourself to spell

        ⇨   *Look at the word; say it to yourself.*

LOOK   ⇨   *If you have difficulties remembering how to write it, trace it with your finger.*

        ⇨   *See if it looks the way it sounds.*

        ⇨   *Mark the bit of the word that causes you difficulties.*

COVER   ⇨   *Shut your eyes: see if you can see the word in your head. do this for at least 13 seconds.*

        ⇨   *If you can't see it in your head, say the word to yourself, and see if the sound reminds you of how it looks.*

        ⇨   *If that doesn't work, look again at the word and say*

REMEMBER   *it in a way that will remind you of how it is spelled. Exaggerate it. Pronounce the bits separately – but remember how it is spelled.*

WRITE   ⇨   *Cover the word: write it from memory. Try and see the word in your head as you write.*

        ⇨   *If you're not sure about it, look at it again.*

CHECK   ⇨   *Check back to see if you got it right. If you didn't, do it again.*

        ⇨   *Later in the day, write it again from memory. If you're not sure of it, look it up before you try.*

REMEMBER

LOOK
COVER
REMEMBER
WRITE
CHECK

best visually, and those that are of most use if they learn best by sound.

> **The teacher's job is not to correct mistakes the pupils has already made, but to help them not to make that mistake next time**

3.2 TEACHING POINTS

Help learners to develop confidence in their spelling by reminding them constantly of this basic procedure:

> **See the word**
>
> **Hear it and pronounce it**
>
> **Write it from memory**

This process uses three memories:
- the visual, through the seeing;
- the auditory, through the hearing and saying;
- the physical 'muscle memory' through the writing.

Draw the learner's attention to the patterns of spelling, and show how to analyse words. As you use the basic approach, remember these principles:

> **Guarantee success**
>
> **Syllabify**
>
> **Give positive advice only**
>
> **Avoid confusing learners**
>
> **Encourage word analysis**

Guarantee success.
Where learners have failed consistently, remove their feeling of failure by giving a series of short regular lessons, designed to produce success – for instance, three simple words daily if the learners are aged 6–8, four for the 9–11 range and six for the 11–14 children. Make sure the learners *succeed*: establish a learning approach which they are confident about using. Set out to convince them they can spell, not to confirm that they can't. Talk about the words

afterwards, and help them to talk about other words like these.

Syllabify
When you are talking about words, it generally helps if you break them into suitable units, usually syllables, to show how they are constructed. This often makes them more memorable than the whole word is:

> caravan = ca-ra-van or car-a-van

Remember **7±**. A long "hard" word may have many more than nine letters:

> *unnecessary* = 11 letters
> *disappointed* = 12 letters

Inexperienced writers can find the length of the word intimidating, and may well cope by copying the word letter by letter. But syllabifying the word into chunks makes a difference:

> *un + ne + cess + ary* = 4 chunks
> *dis + ap + point + ed* = 4 chunks

It is easier for learners to remember a number of simple short syllables, each of which is familiar or simple to spell, rather than one long word. This is especially important with prefixes and suffixes:

> *care-ful-ly*

Teaching like this helps learners to understand the patterns of spelling. You are stressing not how difficult the whole word is (*photograph*) but how easy it is when it is broken down into syllables (*pho-to-graph*).

Syllabifying also demonstrates to the learner that there are logical patterns at work in English spelling. Words which are unconnected semantically can be related by sound or by spelling:

> *pic-ture*   *o-pin-ion*
> *frac-ture*   *on-ion*
> *tor-ture*

Many common errors can be helped by perceiving their syllabic base. The two words *absence* and *present* for instance are often misspelled as *abscence* and *prescence*. Perhaps there is an unconscious analogy drawn with *scent* or *descent*. Show first how the two root words are *absent* and *present*, and how the familiar word *sent* occurs when you syllabify – *ab-sent*, *pre-sent*.

Give positive advice only!
Only give positive advice, not negative. So, for instance, to teach *separate*, draw attention to the

string -para- `Like parade', or comment on the pattern of '*par*' as being 'part of *part*'. Avoid saying 'Don't use an "e" and make it *seperate*.' Wrong examples only confuse learners, especially those who may already have difficulties with words, so never give an incorrect example as a teaching point.

Good spellers, on the other hand, often enjoy searching for exceptions and incorrect examples, because they can see what's wrong.

Avoid confusing learners

For example the common errors – *there, their, they're* – are rarely misspelled: they are spelled perfectly correctly but used in the wrong place. Don't try to teach them together, because that will guarantee confusion. Instead:

Teach *there* with *here, where*
Teach *their* with *your, our*
Teach *they're* with *I'm, she's, you're, we're.*
A useful method is to use *frames*, that is sentences with blanks to be filled in.
❏ Where are they? _____ on the table.
   [*They're*]
❏ Where are you going? I'm going _____. [*there*]
❏ Whose book is that? You know the Smiths? It's _____. [*theirs*]

Encourage word analysis

It can help learners to know that words can contain other words:
❏ An island *is-land*
❏ Breakfast *breaks your fast.*

It can become a game too. Spot the inside words:
❏ Practice – *act, ice*
❏ Cemetery – *met, meter.*

Analysis of this playful kind is the beginning of language study. A simple but effective word study is to invite learners simply to look at a word and say anything they notice about it. At first, answers will be stilted, but accept all observations without comment. As they discover how to look, and what to look at, learners will see more and more patterns and draw more and more analogies. (You can do this with learners of any age.) Here is an example of a class of 12 year olds, invited to comment on the word *talk.*

It's got a *k*
It starts with *t.*
You don't pronounce the *l.*

It's like *stalk.*
It's written with *a*, but you don't say it how it looks (How do you say it? asks the teacher) – like *or.*
It sounds the same as *cork.*
It sounds as if there's an *r* in it.

Can you think of other words like this? asks the teacher.
   Walk ... Fork ...
The words you choose can introduce new patterns, invite complex investigations of, for example, homophones, unusual vowel sounds, *y* used as a vowel, and so on. Anything which helps learners to look closely at words is good.

3.3 DISCOVERING WHICH WORDS TO TEACH

Essentially, the very best way of helping people to improve their spelling is to use the words that they want to employ in their writing; but everyone who provides instruction will want at some time to have access to lists of words. There are many published schemes which provide lists, but all of them have the same limitation – that the words may not be those that learners ever want to use in their own writing, but are more like vocabulary lists in learning a foreign language. Moreover, there is also the risk that if you use someone else's published list, you may unconsciously feel that your job ends there and that the learners will learn just by working through the list. If you collect your own lists, you will be much more sensitive and alert to the real needs of your learners.

All the methods advocated here follow the same principle: the writing is studied, and learners' errors and miscues are collected and analysed by grouping them into families. This process is illuminating for the teacher, and almost certainly ensures that the words used for instruction are relevant and useful for the writers. The first three methods below are the best, but take time. The fourth is quicker, but is liable to the problem identified above – that the words may not be part of the learners' writing vocabulary.

Ideally, treat each learner as an individual with his or her own list of words to be studied and learnt; but that is almost impossible when the learner is one of a large class. So any teaching list will be a compromise between the needs of the individual and those of the larger group.

Remember that if writers can spell most words successfully when they are writing, then it's probably a waste of your time to be teaching them: teach the ones who need it. Some key points to remember in all cases, as you are creating lists:
❏ Choose words the learner is already close to getting right
❏ Choose words which it is important to spell correctly
❏ Choose words which fit in with a group of similar words.

Method 1: Collecting errors from writing

Examine the learners' writing, and collect a hundred spelling errors. In a class, you can use the work of three or four children, spanning the ability range; but children under nine may not write much, and so you will probably need more than three or four children's work to make up the 100 words.

Classify the miscues as suggested in Chapter 4, *Analysis* and prepare a teaching strategy to deal with the spellings and patterns revealed – though remember the warning on page 34.

Method 2: Collecting words asked for

Make your own list of the words that learners ask for while they are writing. This is a very good indication of what they really want to spell. If certain words recur frequently, prepare word cards, a wall-sheet, or a list or database on your computer. Your word-book (see p 45) is a good source for these words.

This list won't tell you where they would make a mistake if they tried to spell themselves, or the kind of miscues they will make; so it's best to add the collection of words from Method 1 to this list.

Method 3: Listing known problems

Spend time asking the learners to tell you the words they know they find difficult, for you to list. You can use this list both for spelling instruction and for general discussion of the words or parts of words that cause the problems. Every so often, you can distribute the list and check which words are still causing difficulties, which new ones they would wish to add (for example from other lessons in school, or words they have met in their reading and writing), and which they can now spell. You can

prepare lists of words you know they will meet in other lessons, so they are ready for them.

Method 4: Creating study lists

Use one of the various spelling lists published, and dictate it to the group or individual. The learners leave a dash if they do not know how to spell a word. The words that are omitted form the words lists for study and learning, and if a word is spelled incorrectly, that word is also added to the learning list to be studied.

Remember that it is not only the spelling of individual words that you are trying to teach, but the basic spelling patterns, so that learners can spell correctly words they have not been taught but want to write. The aim is for the learners not to have to memorise individual words, but to be able to work them out from known patterns and principles.

> **If you are collecting words for analysis and use spelling lists, do not give learners marks. It is important that they should understand that they are not being tested to see how ignorant they are, but that you are trying, with their help, to create a resource bank that will help them to become good spellers. It is a joint effort.**

These sections, 3.1 to 3.3, have dealt with methods of teaching spelling, and have involved thinking quite carefully about what one is to do before actually doing it. What comes next will be a more practical set of ideas for what to do with learners.

3.4 ORGANISATION AT DIFFERENT LEARNING STAGES

Everything the experienced adult does to help a young learner is designed to help learners to become confident enough to write lucidly and effectively, without anxiety or indecision. This section outlines activities and approaches which will help the learners to become confident. I have associated the ideas with particular ages, but you will need to be sensitive to the stage the learners you are dealing with have reached, remembering the Gentry stages outlined in Section 1.1. Recognise that some older learners will be insecure and may well need approaches which appear to be more appropriate to younger children before they become confident enough to work at the level which fits their chronological age.

*E*arly stages (for children aged 3–5)

Expect these children to be at a Pre-communicative stage, where they are just coming to terms with print and how it works.

Encourage all attempts to play with the letters of the alphabet, using plastic or wooden letters, chalk on chalk boards, writing in sand, and any other way possible.

Point out to learners **how their names are made up of the letters of the alphabet**.

Use letter names (the traditional A-B-C) as well as letter sounds.

Stress the sounds that letters make together, pronouncing the consonant with its attendant vowel, not on its own.

Encourage, praise, and draw attention to **the use of letters in drawings and paintings**.

*C*hildren aged 5–7

Expect these children to be at the Semi-phonetic stage, although there will begin to be wide variation between individuals.

Spend no longer than ten minutes at a time on direct spelling lessons, but **comment on words at all times**.

Encourage children to write out **words they know and want to celebrate, using word processors**.

Discuss children's invented spellings with them, helping them to articulate the logic of the rules they have applied.

When children are writing:

❑ always **encourage them to try a word**: it might be right;

❑ if they are uncertain about a word, suggest they **put the first letter and a line (b_____)** or just a line if they are not sure of the first letter. When you read the piece, discuss the proper spelling of the word with them;

❑ **encourage the use of suitable dictionaries**. Some children may prefer to look up words after they have written, while others will want to look them up during the writing;

❑ **encourage them to act as proof readers** for each others' writing. It is always easier to spot spelling miscues in someone else's writing than in one's own. Notice when the children can recognise miscues and self-correct.

Every two or three weeks: **collect words** that the children have misspelled in their current writing, and **use them as the basis for test-teaching**. Dictate five words to the children, and then show the correct spelling. The children then learn the words they did not spell correctly, for a retest of the same words. Choose two kinds of word:

❑ those that many of the children regularly misspell;

❑ those that raise useful teaching points.

With children who find spelling difficult, you may need to do this more regularly, though be sensitive about drawing unnecessary attention to them, and never describe these children as in any way "failing".

*F*or children aged 7–11

Expect these children to range from the Semi-phonetic to the Phonetic stages, with most attempts to spell being reasonable phonic alternatives.

Use all the above ideas, adjusted for the age of children, but in addition:

❑ **have brief regular lessons** (ten minutes once a week) in which you introduce some feature of spelling appropriate to the level the children have reached, and the work they are doing at the time. For example, you might choose the suffix -*ly* and its effect:

  usual+*ly* = usually

 or a prefix *un*- and its effect:

  un + *necessary* + *ly* = unnecessarily.

 Notice how the y changes to i.

❑ **Encourage the use of spell-checkers**, either free-standing ones or on word-processors, for children to find out what is wrong with a high-lighted word.

Some people worry that spell-checkers will stop children from learning to spell. In fact, though, just as you have to understand numbers to use a calculator properly, so a child has to understand spelling to be able to use a spell checker properly.

❏ Introduce word history and families of words, and relate spelling to language study in general (see Chapter 7)

Children aged 11–16

Expect the range to be very wide, all the way from semi-phonetic to correct spelling.

As children grow older and become more experienced, the range inevitably becomes greater, and one set of teaching words or lessons will be unlikely to cover all needs. Teachers who work with older children may expect that correcting children's written work will be sufficient to teach the correct spelling. But in fact, to be effective you will need to individualise spelling instruction.

❏ Use the collection of students' words (as explained in the previous section) at least once a month to **select a repertoire of words** for test-teaching.

❏ In marking students' work, always **give explanations for corrections**, and relate them to a pattern or to analogous words.

❏ **If you offer rules, make sure they work**. For example the effect of *-e* at the end of words is not consistent. It works for *make* and *site* but not for *give* or *were*. And what about live (= inhabit) and live (=not dead)?

❏ **Encourage students to construct their own rules**. Set regular but brief exercises in which they have to propose a rule which covers a specified spelling pattern. For example:

    fly   flies
    sky   skies

Find other words which fit the pattern. (See also *Discovering Rules* on p.53)

Adults and young adults

All instruction should be individualised as much as possible, unless the adults *choose* to work with others. By this age, if people have problems with spelling, they are likely to have a low self-image and to lack confidence in themselves as writers and as spellers. Whatever else you do, you should set out to develop self confidence, and to rid them of fear.

Use the ideas outlined above for 11-16 year olds, and in addition, those that follow:

❏ Discuss the kinds of writing the learner wants to be able to do.

❏ Discuss the learner's view of him- or herself as a writer and speller, and discover together whether you need to use an approach that stresses the *visual*, the *auditory* or *rote memory*. (Different approaches may be valuable for different words.)

❏ Use words that you both know the learner wants to spell.

❏ Encourage attention to environmental literacy – words around us all the time – and especially to 'social sight words' – that is, words often seen in public places, which it is important to understand and spell.

❏ Use dictionaries freely, and explain how they work.

❏ Remember the advice that Catherine Moorhouse gives:

> **Don't ask students to learn a word without showing them a way of doing it.**

3.5 TEACHING IDEAS AND GAMES

The basic teaching strategies outlined so far do the teaching: the ideas in this section support the teaching, providing ways of investigating and playing with words. But they also involve one or other of the basic principles of learning to spell, and many learners will take them over for themselves, and use them as part of their personal strategies for learning to spell.

Words on cards

This is best done as group work, for learners of all ages. Select appropriate words, and prepare them written large on card. For younger children, flash-card games are useful for introducing words which children will use in various subjects – Maths, for example. Remember that the flash-card helps only with the spelling, not the meaning.

1. Say the word, and show the card for thirteen seconds, making sure that everyone can see it clearly. The length of time is, of course, important because of the duration of short-term memory (see page 44).

2. Cover the card. The learners are asked to remember the word, and think of it, for another ten seconds or so.

3. They write the word down, and then compare

what they have written with each other. If necessary, they discuss what they have written, and come to a conclusion which is correct.

4. You show them the original card as a way of checking.

You can emphasise the 'hard spots' of the word, by underlining, colouring, or some other strategy.

Learners are practising visualising, and supporting each other in the process. They must remember the word and carry it in the head for some time, and so write from their mental image of the word.

Flash cards are simple technology, and some may prefer to use overhead projectors, computers, and other equipment. The medium is less important than the process followed.

You can do the same thing with phrases rather than individual words. The learners have to work harder, because they are remembering a string of words rather than a string of letters. Use a phrase or sentence that makes sense, not just a string of unconnected words, and include words that you feel will most benefit the learners. The discussion afterwards should draw attention to the generalisations you feel are important: a phrase like *The sun is really shining* gives you the chance to talk about single and double letters; the effect of *-ly* on *real*; and the effects of *-ing* on words with an e-marker.

Word families and dictionary work

This is best for individual and pair work. These are just starter ideas, and you will be able to devise your own similar exercises.

Word families and patterns
❑ Find words in this list which have the same two or more letters next to each other in the same order, and mark them. You'll find there is more than one set of letters.

flies	*there*
dried	*where*
blood	*head*
field	*form*
from	*files*

❑ Arrange these words in dictionary order

(a)	*arrow*	*game*
	yard	*from*
	silver	*train*
(b)	*ready*	*rock*
	read	*rabbit*

robber	*remain*
rude	*rage*

These represent two extremes of difficulty: the first involves only initial letters, the second involves going to the fourth or fifth letter to decide on alphabetical order.

Dictionary games

Depending on the age, stage and experience of the learners, you can design different games and exercises which raise important points about language in general and spelling in particular. Adjust your exercises to what you know is appropriate to the dictionaries the learners use. (More general points about dictionaries are made in the next section.) Do use a decent dictionary: it is frustating when learners find that their dictionaries simply do not include words they want to use and spell. Some examples of games follow:

❑ The simplest game helps learners to become familiar with alphabetical order, with how to use facilities like head words, and with the general issue of where in a dictionary they are likely to find a word. You say a word: the players have to find it. This can be played by individuals, by pairs with the same dictionary, or by groups with a dictionary each. You can handicap so that some groups find one word, others find another.

❑ Find 5 words beginning with a particular group of letters; for example ps- *(psalm, pseudo, psychiatrist, psychic, psycho-)*, or chr- *(Christmas, chrome, chronicle, chronometer, chrysalis)*

❑ Find as many words as possible up to 10 (depending on age) with a common element eg *comm- (command, commit, committee, commence, comment, commission, common, communist, communicate, community)*.

❑ Start with one base word, and see how many other words you can create from that root:
fear: *fearless, fearful, feared, fearing*
join: *joined, joiner, joint, joining, disjointed, conjoin*
story: *stories, historical, story-teller.*

Using nonsense words

Games like the ones that follow demonstrate the relationship between sound and symbol, which must be understood if one is to become a competent speller. Learners have to use both visual and auditory memories to find logical and convincingly English patterns of symbols to fit the sounds heard. You affirm the underlying logic of English spelling:
❑ there *are* patterns and families;

❏ the particular sounds may have different ways of being written down;

❏ there are only a limited number of ways, and they do obey certain 'rules'.

Ask the group to spell a nonsense word that you say. Construct the nonsense words to fit what you know to be the most useful patterns for the learners. So you might have a group who have difficulty with the single-double problem, and offer them:

    linning   grining   frumy   bolly

Accept any answer, but ask for some explanation as to why the learner has offered that spelling, and insist they include real words that they know are spelled like that. The discussion might go like this:

> You ask for the spelling of *frimble*
>
> A learner offers *frimbal.*
>
> You ask the rest of the group for comments. Draw their attention to *-bal* and ask for examples of real words which sound the same as *frimble.*
>
> List their spellings yourself as the learners offer them, without asking how they are spelled. Look them up, if you're not sure: it is important they see these words correctly instead of getting confused over variant spellings.

They may offer, for example:

nimble	*cymbal*
thimble	*symbol*
Wimbledon	
Dimbleby	

You ask: Which seems the most likely spelling? (in this case obviously *-ble*).

Learners can make up their own nonsense words, and must be able to justify why they think it should be spelled the way they have spelled it.

An alternative is to invite as many different spellings of a single nonsense word:

    nope   reakage   casitude   foumal

Discuss the suggested spellings, decide which are the most likely, and make lists of real words which fit the pattern:

nope	*noap*	*gnope*
rope	*soap*	*gnome*
mope	*boat*	

Discovering rules

As I say in *The main myth – spelling rules* (p.72), when learners derive their own rules, then they begin to identify the principles of English spelling. Setting puzzles that encourage learners to make rules is a powerful way for them to make their own generalisations. You can obviously prepare examples of varying difficulty. You provide groups of words like these: the learners have to work out what the pattern is:

Quiet, queue, quite, quickly: What's the pattern?
[Answer – *q+u followed by a vowel*]

Making, caring, smiling, shaking   What's the pattern?
[Answer – *-e dropped before an ending*]

Slamming, hitting, running, tapping What's the pattern?
[Answer – *the final consonant doubled before a suffix*]

Theirs, ours, yours, his, hers   What's the pattern?
[Answer - *belonging to them, us... An -s is added*]

Games

1. *Hangman* Hangman is well known as a spelling game, and there are some interesting computer versions. But it is less useful than it should be, because it is usually played as a guessing game. Much better is the next game.

2. *Shannon's Game* A game called after the man who invented it for research purposes in order to explore the predictability of words.

You put a number of dashes to represent the number of letters in the word. (If you wish, or you feel the learners need the support, then put the first letter; but it's more fun if you don't.) Thus you present (on the chalk-board, the overhead projector screen, or the computer screen) this:

    – – – – – –

The players must guess the letters one by one, beginning with the first. Count and record the guesses. After ten guesses, if they haven't guessed, tell them what the first letter is:

    c _ _ _ _ _

The next letter is also hard because there are still lots of options:

    c h - - - -

They will find the next letter in this word easier. They will probably guess *a, e, i, o, u,* and if they're not yet right, follow with *r* (*chr-*) or, with older players, *chl-.*

    c h u _ _ _

The next stage produces as guesses *c, b, m, n* etc. When they are certain, not just guessing, they complete the word:

    c h u r c h.

The point of the game is that without necessarily being conscious of it at first, the players inevitably apply to the guesses their knowledge, explicit or implicit, of the structure of English spelling. If anyone makes wild random guesses, note who it is: they will need closer attention.

The game indicates the predictability of certain spelling structures and letter strings. Discussion of the number of guesses recorded, and why the chosen letters were suggested, can be used to point out the different kinds of letter order, and to talk about alternative words that were possible at different stages. Talk about how likely the letters were, which were just guess work or genuine prediction, which words they had in mind, and so on. This is the beginning of rule-making and generalisation. As you continue to play the game, learners become more sophisticated and more aware of patterns and how predictable they are.

3. *Growing words* For individuals, pairs or groups. A word is written, and one of its letters is used as the beginning of the next one. For younger children, use short (3–4 letter) words to begin with, and start the new word with the last letter:

> *new*
>> *wall*
>>> *link*
>>>> *king* etc

As learners become more confident, any letter after the first can begin the next word, but then the new word must include all the remaining letters:

> *new*
>> *ewe*
>>> *went*
>>>> *enter*
>>>>> *tern* etc

4. *Ghosts* An excellent, if rather complex game, which many groups become quite obsessively interested in.

❏ Divide the group into teams of 3-4.

❏ The teacher writes on the board and is neutral judge, scorer and ultimate arbiter. Have a good dictionary available to settle rows, and a stop watch or egg timer handy, otherwise the game lasts for ever.

❏ Team 1 says a letter which is the first letter of a word they have in mind. They say, for instance, *b.* They do not say what the word is, unless challenged (see below).

❏ The next team, with a word in mind beginning with b – which may or may not be the original word team 1 were thinking of – adds a letter. They say for example *b e –.* Incidentally, a good deal of the pleasure of this game comes from

taking something which looks as though it must inevitably be one word, and suddenly producing an unexpected twist which confuses everyone else.

❏ The smallest allowable word has three letters. The team which completes a word loses a point. Thus if team 3, thinking of *beef* adds an *e,* they have completed a word – *bee* – and lose a point; but only if another team spots it and challenges them. Names of people and places and abbreviations are not allowed. But words like *jack,* which are names but also things, are allowed. This is where you'll need the dictionary.

❏ Put a time limit on a team's deliberations – say 30 seconds.

❏ Since teams are trying not to complete a word, but to force another team to do it, sometimes they invent words to wriggle out. If a following team thinks there is no such word, they may say "Challenge!" The last team then has to say the word they had in mind. If the umpire (ie you) accepts it, then the challenging team loses a point. If not, the challenged lose a point. Any spelling error can also be challenged: if a word has been spelled wrongly and is challenged, the *last* team loses a point, not the team that misspelled it originally. A team that is challenged and has a real word in mind, but misspells it, loses.

❏ Three points lose a life, and the team is then a ghost, and is out.

❏ Enthusiasts aged 11 and over can be introduced to *Superghosts,* in which letters can be added at either end of the word; and then to *Supersuperghosts,* which includes hyphens.

I admit cheerfully that I stole this game from James Thurber, who also came up with two excellent puzzlers for players of Supersuperghosts, when he asked which two familiar words are these parts of:

> *ug-ug*
> *ach-ach*

(Answers at the end of the chapter.)

A cautionary note on games

Anagrams and crosswords are well-known, but generally don't teach spelling. They give good spellers a chance to use their skill, but may depress a poor speller. However, if you give learners the clues, and the answers, not in order, then they have to read carefully, match words to meanings, and fit words together in the puzzle.

As far as possible, all games for teaching spelling should involve writing, and not be only oral. Only very good spellers – and sometimes not even they – can easily spell orally. Games which pressurise weak spellers by making them write words quickly are not good for them.

A good spelling game is one that stresses visual patterns, and makes it clear to players that there are predictable patterns which they can anticipate.

3.6 DICTIONARIES

Using dictionaries does not itself teach anyone how to spell; but someone whose spelling is uncertain finds it hard to use dictionaries at all. There is an assumption that dictionary use is a skill which is simply acquired. It is not, of course: some will acquire it, but many have to be helped to learn it. You won't miraculously ensure perfect spelling by helping pupils to use dictionaries, but you will find that it's time well spent.

Catherine Hilton and Margaret Hyder suggest that the basic dictionary skills are:
❑ Using an alphabetic sequence (and indeed, knowing the alphabet)
❑ Working out the beginning of words
❑ Working through words
❑ Saying the word
❑ Scanning skills
❑ Understanding an entry.

To which, Heilmann, an American researcher, added:
❑ the knowledge that words can mean different things
❑ a knowledge of root words and their various derivations
❑ an understanding that letters and combinations of letters have different sound values in different contexts.

To those lists, I would add:
❑ a familiarity with the commonest ways of symbolising sounds.

A dictionary user, faced with looking up a word of unknown spelling, ought to have some idea of where to start looking, with a fair degree of success. To do this, we need to know something about the probability of sounds being symbolised in one way rather than another, and which is the most likely way for this set of sounds to be written. Thus,

learners may need to be introduced to common variants, especially at the beginnings of words:

Sound	Initial symbol
f	f/ph
k	c/k/ch
j	j/g
n	n/kn/gn/pn/mn
r	r/wr
s	s/c/ps
w	w/wh

Choice becomes more complex once we consider vowels: the sound of the diphthong *a* can be symbolised in several different ways:

a-	able
ai	daily (in the middle of words)
ay	day (at the end of words)
a-e	make
ei	neighbour, weight
au	gauge
ey	they (unusual)

But what's important is that learners should know that there are alternatives, and that some are more probable than others.

Dictionaries themselves have their own conventions which learners have to know about, and not just the apparently baffling abbreviations, but much more basic and useful conventions. Not everyone realises, for instance, that the two words printed at the head of a page tell you something about the alphabetic range of the words on that page. The head word at the left gives the first word on the page, that on the right gives the last main entry; and they indicate that between them comes the range of words that will appear on that page.

Experienced dictionary users know something that they may not have made explicit to themselves. They take it for granted that the entries are alphabetic, and know of course that *p* comes after *n*; but what they may not explicitly realise is that they have a pretty good idea when they open the dictionary itself that they will be somewhere fairly close to the section they want. They do this because they have learnt through experience that each letter has a different number of entries, rather than an equal number. In effect, a dictionary can be divided into four parts which often look like this:

Part One   A – E Contains 5 sections – longest section = C
Part Two   F – M Contains 8 sections – longest section = F or M

Part Three N - R Contains 5 sections – longest section = P
Part Four S - Z Contains 8 sections – longest section = S

The experienced user, then, looking for a word beginning with *P* will tend automatically to open the dictionary about half way, and will then skim quickly to find the proper place after that. Because each section contains at least one letter with a long entry, that gives the user another clue about finding the best way to the wanted word.

A count in the Concise Oxford Dictionary gives a useful indication of the relative frequency of English words by their first letter. The first ten, by the number of pages under each letter, look like this:

Order	Letter	Number of pages
1.	S	211
2.	C	135
3	P	129
4	T	95
5	R	88
6	B	82
7	A	81
8	D	78
9	M	67
10	F	65

Finally, the learner has to find out what the style of the dictionary is. Does *accountable* come under the general entry for *account* or is it a separate entry on its own?

3.7 HANDWRITING

Because spelling only exists when people write, and should never be taught independently of writing, it is not surprising that there should be a relationship between handwriting and spelling. The relationship works at various levels.

❑ Correctly formed, connected handwriting helps learners to practise letter strings and to generate the 'muscle memory' that is so important in fluent, accurate spelling;

❑ Therefore, right from the beginning handwriting practice should always involve writing words or letter strings, not individual letters;

❑ A learner's handwriting can also illuminate their approach to spelling. A writer who hesitates in the middle of writing because he or she is unsure of the spelling will 'disrupt the flow of their handwriting', as Rosemary Sasson puts it. Be alert to examples of this: it may demonstrate, more clearly than the learner can explain, when exactly he or she is having difficulties.

FUSTET

FUSTET, *n. fus*-tet, young fustic, the sumac. *Rhus coriaria*, the leaves of which are used for tanning and for producing a yellow dye. (Fr.)
FUSTIAN, *n. fust*-yan, a kind of coarse thick twilled cotton cloth ; an inflated style of writing : bombast : *a*. made of fustian ; swelling above the dignity of the thoughts or subject ; ridiculously tumid ; bombastic. (Fustat, a suburb of Cairo, where fustian was first made.)
FUSTIANIST, *n. fust*-yan-ist, one who writes bombast.
FUSTIC, *n. fus*-tik, the wood of *Chlorophora tinctoria*, a tropical American tree which affords a dingy yellow dye. (Fr. *fustoc*.)
FUSTIGATE, *v.t. fus*-te-gate, to beat with a cudgel. Fustigated. Fustigates. Fustigating. (L. *fustigatus*, clubbed.)
FUSTIGATION, *n. fus*-te-*gay*-shon, cudgelling.
FUSTILARIAN, *n. fus*-te-*lare*-e-an, a low fellow ; a scoundrel.
FUSTILUG, *n. fus*-te-lug, a gross, fat, unwieldy person.
FUSTINESS, *n. fus*-te-ness, a fusty state or quality ; ill smell from mouldiness, or mouldiness itself.
FUSTY, *a. fus*-te, mouldy ; ill-smelling.
FUSURE, *n. few*-sjure, a smelting ; a fusion.
FUTCHEL, *n. futch*-el, the beam along the bottom of a carriage which supports the pole and splinter-bar.
FUTHORC, *n. footh*-ork, the Runic alphabet, so called from the first six letters, *f*, *u*, *th*, *o*, *r*, *k*, the *th* being thorn, the English theta.
FUTILE, *a. few*-tile, trifling ; useless ; of no avail. (Fr.)
FUTILELY, *ad. few*-tile-le, in a futile manner.
FUTILITY, *n. few*-til-e-te, worthlessness ; uselessness.
FUTTOCKS, *n.pl. fut*-toks, the middle division of a ship's timbers, situated between the floor and the upper timbers [Naut.] ; foot-hooks. Futtock plates, certain iron plates, the upper parts of which are open like a ring, and used to fix the dead-eyes in. Futtock shrouds, the short shrouds running inwards to the mast from the futtock plates above [Naut.].

FYRDUNG

FUTURE, *a. few*-tewr, that is to come ; *n*. time to come. Future perfect, expressing the past in reference to an assumed future. Future tense, the modification of a verb which expresses a future act or event [Gram.]. (O.Fr. *futur*.)
FUTURELY, *ad. few*-tewr-le, in time to come.
FUTURISM, *n. few*-tewr-ism, rejection of customary usage and adoption of ancient failures as new departures ; a secessionist movement in Art that began in Italy in 1910-11, and spread gradually over Western Europe.
FUTURIST, *n. few*-tewr-ist, a practiser of futurism ; one who has regard to the future ; one who maintains that the scriptural prophecies have yet to be fulfilled [Theol.] ; pertaining to futurism.
FUTURITION, *n. few*-tewr-*ish*-on, the state of being to come hereafter.
FUTURITY, *n. few-tewr*-it-e, future time ; time to come ; event to come ; the state of being yet to come.
FUZE. *n. fewze*, a fuse.
FUZEE, *n. few*-zee, fusee.
FUZZ, *n. fuz*, fine, light particles ; loose, volatile matter : *v.i.* to fly off in minute particles. Fuzzed. Fuzzes. Fuzzing.
FUZZ-BALL, *n. fuz*-bawl, a puff ball, a species of *Lycoperdon* or *Bovista*.
FUZZLE, *v.t. fuz*-zl, to intoxicate. Fuzzled. Fuzzles. Fuzzling.
FUZZY, *a. fuz*-ze, shaggy ; woolly ; blurred.
FY, *int. fi*, a word which expresses dislike, disapprobation, blame, abhorrence, or contempt ; fie !
FYKE, *n. fike*, a long bag-net. (Dut. *fuik*, net.)
FYLFOT, *n. fil*-fot, a rectangular cross with the arms bent at right angles, often used in decoration and embroidery during the middle ages ; the swastika, or hammer of Thor.
FYRD, *n. furd*, the full military force of the nation. (A.S.)
FYRDUNG, *n. furd*-ung, an array, at the command of the king, of all able to bear arms. (A.S.)

A page out of a dictionary

❏ For older learners, the tension they feel about their real or imagined inadequacies in spelling will show through their handwriting.

The problem of handwriting is greater with younger learners, because they are learning general muscle control as well as learning to shape letters in the ways that are necessary, that is:

❏ straight letters start at the top;

❏ round letters go anti-clockwise;

❏ all letters should have exit strokes, (preparing for joined-up writing).

Margaret Peters reminds us to *observe* young people writing, to learn about how they approach it, and suggests that there are only two basic rules of handwriting, as indicated above; and that they can be explained to children like this:

❏ Begin at the top of the letter.

❏ Go this way round –

Unexpectedly, research with younger children (say, up to about 9) shows that carefulness in handwriting tends to produce swiftness, rather than slowness, because it leads to a fluent hand. Slow handwriting tends often to go along with spelling that is worse, while rapid, careful writing – that is, well-formed and legible writing – is associated with accurate spelling. As children grow older, speed is an increasing priority. One of the most important things to learn is that different handwriting is appropriate for different purposes.

❏ If the writer is the only one who needs to read it, then as long as he or she can read it, that is all that matters;

❏ If someone else is to read it, then the writer has to have a concern for the reader, and the legibility will be different;

❏ If the writing is to be a proper presentation, then almost certainly it will not be the first draft that is presented, but a worked-on version.

Notice the hesitations and deletions in the word, and the difference between this word and the handwriting of the following words.

The 'C' is an insertion: notice that the girl appears to have rested her pen on the 'o' – while she was thinking?

"Then I wondered around the room, knocking your stuff on the floor by accident," said the strange man.

She has traced over the final letter, and there is another mark of the pen resting after the word – another thinking or checking time

11-year-old girl

In summary, children and adults alike should be encouraged to have several levels of handwriting, and be clear about when each is appropriate.

3.8 DOING CORRECTIONS

> **The teacher's job is not to correct mistakes the pupils have already made, but to *help them not to make that mistake next time***

The commonest way in which school pupils are asked to correct their spelling is to write out errors a number of times. This does not improve their spelling, however, because repetitive copying bypasses the use of visual memory. Margaret Peters (1974), reflecting on her research, pointed out the difference between rote correction technique, where children copy out mistakes, and 'rational techniques, where the teacher has worked out a way for children to correct their mistakes autonomously, drawing attention to 'hard spots' within words. She found that 'three quarters of the classes which make least progress are taught by ...rote techniques, and three quarters of the classes which make most progress are taught by teachers pursuing *rational* correction techniques.'

Some preliminary points

❑ Don't mark every miscue or misspelling. Choose three or four at most and pick the ones that most need correcting – that is, words the learner ought to be able to spell at this stage, or is nearly able to spell, and words which *generalise*. Relate your corrections to what you know of the learner's general approach to spelling and learning.

❑ I wrote 'words the learner ought to be able to spell'. But this is not as simple as it sounds. Some writers will know that some words cause difficulty, and will ask for help with them; but they might also think that they are spelling some words correctly that they are, in fact, misspelling. Be aware that some learners may simply not be able to proof-read their own work, because they may think, for instance, that *latter* is the correct way to spell *later*. An important way of helping learners is occasionally to list for them all the miscues you have found, writing them not in the incorrect form but clearly and correctly, and ask the learners to study them as for the basic approach (see page 44).

❑ Marking a writer's errors should *always* be less important than reading with sympathy and understanding what he or she is trying to say.
❑ Tolerate learners who cross out frequently during their writing. It is always best to have the whole word written, rather than have letters inserted.

Some suggested ways of encouraging spelling corrections

1. Often a writer who reads their work aloud will pick out the errors as he or she reads. This is probably because during the process of writing, the focal attention of the writer is always on the substance and content, and not on its appearance, which is subsidiary during the act of composition. During the reading aloud, the reader focuses on each word, and is more likely to spot an error.

As long as the writer is a good enough reader, these errors will be caught in proof-reading. You can try giving the writing back and saying, 'You've made three (or whatever) spelling mistakes there. Can you find them?' But only do that if the writer is likely to find them; that is, if he or she is potentially at least a good speller.

2. When you are working on a learner's writing, do not insert letters in a misspelled word. It can confuse the writer. Instead try one of these approaches:
❑ Write the correct form on a separate piece of paper, or in the margin in pencil. (If the learner is left-handed, write the word in the right hand margin.) The writer can erase the misspelling and insert the correct spelling. Your word can then be erased, and the page looks unmarked.
❑ Delete the wrong word completely. Write in the whole of the correct version in pencil, either above the deletion or in the margin.
❑ If a learner writes out the words somewhere else – say in their word book – they can use felt-tips to colour the part or parts of the word that cause difficulty.
❑ A very simple and effective approach for the teacher is to comment on misspellings not to complain about errors, but to praise the attempt by recognising what the writer was trying to do:

'You had a good try and you used the right sounds; it sounds like that but we write it like this.'
❑ Marking the error with a symbol like *sp* or *s* without giving the correct version of the word is unproductive because it merely demonstrates to the writer that he or she has "failed" without

showing how to improve. Remember Eddie who already knew that his spelling was weak. "They keep saying 'You must improve your spelling', but they never tell me *how*."

Many writers, although they find it difficult to tell teachers so, are upset if their work is heavily marked in red or in ink or biro by the teacher, especially if they were pleased with the substance of what they wrote. The intrusive visibility of the marks becomes more important than the original writing. It makes them feel that their voice and ideas are irrelevant: all that apparently matters to the teacher is neatness and spelling.

Be careful therefore that you don't make learners merely feel worse about their spelling. A teacher should be a helper and guide, not a printer's proof-reader.

Although it was published many years ago, Nancy Martin's work *Here, Now and Beyond* [1968] contains useful and helpful comments and ideas about spelling and about encouraging pupils to become competent proof-readers.

Answer to the SuperGhosts question on page 55: *ug-ug* is the centre of *plug-ugly*; *ach-ach* is the centre of *stomach-ache*

Chapter 4

ANALYSIS

The four sections here outline the important processes of considering the writing of learners, in order to see what patterns of invention, miscue and error occur.

4.1   *ANALYSIS begins the chapter by considering the whole process of analysis, with some warnings about expecting easy solutions.*

4.2   *ANALYSIS 1: 100 errors illustrates how to explore the work of a large group, in this case, 9-10 year old children*

4.3   *ANALYSIS 2: a piece of writing looks in detail at the work of Michael, a 9 year old boy.*

4.4   *ANALYSIS 3: a spelling test takes the more threatening experience of a spelling test, and considers Lisa's results to see what we might learn from that.*

4.1 ANALYSIS

I have mentioned in several places the idea of analysing learners' miscues. The analysis of a learner's misspelled words is not just a matter of marking or counting mistakes. It involves trying to see what patterns of invention, miscue and error emerge when the writing is classified. Just as there are families of correctly spelled words, so there tend to be families of error and miscue, generally related to underlying patterns of thinking and beliefs about language and words. By analysing the work of a class, a teacher can teach more economically, more carefully and with more chance of success because it becomes possible to target individuals and at the same time deal with general miscues.

The adult working with a single learner – son, daughter, or pupil – learns from analysis exactly where to begin; and involving the learner in the analysis begins the important process of demystifying spelling for him or her.

All learners have their own patterns but it is not necessary, or desirable, or possible to analyse each learner's errors as thoroughly as these examples do. However, if you want to design a programme for an individual, or to locate someone's strengths and weaknesses, analysis is the best way of doing it.

It will not always be possible to classify all the errors. Some have no apparent logic. But *trying* to classify and understand them will show you a good deal about what is going on for that individual.

> **Spelling errors are not simply mistakes: they are miscues, with reasons for each miscue. Find the reason why the learner spelled the word that way, and there is a chance you can help them not to.**

But there are warnings: whatever the categorisations you choose to use, do not automatically assume that all the misspellings in that category were caused by the same thing. For instance, you decide to look for letters omitted. You find two examples in two scripts by different writers, both for the word clear: one writes *clar*, the other *cler*.

Attention to the surface feature – in this case, a letter omitted – does not necessarily tell you anything significant. Yes, both have one letter omitted; but it is almost certain that there are two quite different explanations for the omission. My personal preference would be to feel that *cler* is less worrying than *clar*, because it is a more reasonable phonic alternative, whereas *clar* is a curious misspelling. Was it hasty writing? Would the writer recognise afterwards what the correct spelling should be?

More significantly, though, what is the pattern within a writer's work? If these two miscues occurred in two different writers, that is one thing; but if they both appeared in the same piece of writing, what then?

Recognise, then, that the reason for the occurrence in people's writing of any particular miscue or style of miscue will vary between individuals.

4.2 ANALYSIS 1: 100 ERRORS FROM A CLASS'S WRITING

One hundred errors were collected from the written work of a class of 9 – 10 year olds. They had been asked to imagine that they were taking a parachute jump, and to write about the experience and their feelings. All the spellings quoted in this section come from the one hundred words collected: the complete list of words is at the end of the section.

*T*he procedure

The purpose of the analysis is to break the errors into different groups so that teaching can be specific. It is the causes of the misspellings that you are looking for: find them and you can help the learners improve. Analysis isolates possible patterns of error which indicate underlying causes.

1. Collect the words by writing down the misspelled form, not the correct form. If there is any possibility of your being puzzled later, note both the misspelling and the correct form eg *hire* (higher), *ball* (bail), *of* (off). Count different misspellings of the same word as different errors, eg *floting, flouting* (floating)

represents two misspellings. Note if the same misspelling occurs more than once, especially if it is in the writing of different learners.

2. Arrange the words in a way you find helpful. I do it alphabetically by error: thus *iys* (eyes) goes under *i* not *e*. You may prefer a different way.

3. When you begin classifying, look for the most obvious groups first. As you eliminate a group of words, patterns begin to emerge, It's at this stage that the work is most interesting and most difficult. You can take over other people's classifications (Margaret Peters suggests some interesting ones in her work (1976)) or devise your own that you feel comfortable with. An example is given on page 35.

4. Not all the words fit easily into categories. Where, for instance, would you put *sleep*? Keep a category for "unclassifiable"; but use it as a last resort. If there are more than 12–15 words in the unclassifiable group, look again, because you have probably put words there that ought to be in a different category.

5. Some words can go in more than one category. Put them in the category of the simplest error, or the one that offers the simplest way in to instruction. Thus, *pesfull* is placed with the group of suffix errors, because the writer may not have recognised that the word is *peace + ful*. If the writer still makes that error after learning about the suffix *-ful*, then consider it as a phonic alternative.

6. Once you have constructed categories, you may see much more clearly what kind of teaching programme is needed. But remember that not all the misspellings in one category are caused by the same underlying factor. *Safly* and *hardle* are both in the *-ly* suffix group; but the writer who spells *safly* seems to understand about the suffix *-ly* and may have simply omitted the *-e*. She is probably potentially a better speller than the child who produces *hardle*, who does not apparently understand that the suffix is *-ly*.

7. Finally, remember that analysing the work of the whole group necessarily produces a whole-group programme, and is unlikely to solve specific problems, for which you need to do an individual analysis. What it will do is to identify those kinds of misspellings that most learners in this group are apparently most likely to make. It probably does not identify individual words to teach. More importantly than that, it points to the patterns that need learning.

Doing this analysis is difficult and takes a continuous stretch of time. Do it systematically. As Margaret Peters's research shows, any systematic approach to spelling, whatever its basis, is better than no approach at all.

Analysis

The one hundred words in this set categorise as follows:

Prefix, suffix

Twenty words, mostly involving suffixes: *-ly, -ful, -ing, -ed*. Also the prefixes *dis-, de-*.

Most of the words concern what happens to the final *-e* if a suffix is added - *lonley, safly, comeing, wakeing*. Because learners are often confused by this, some add an unnecessary *-e-*: *lightley, slowley*. Three errors involve the change of *y* to *i*: *cryed, emptyness, tryed*; others are confused about what the prefix or suffix actually is: - *full* for *-ful, diss-* for *dis-, -d* or *-t* for *-ed* (see pages 66).

Letters omitted or inserted

Sixteen words omit letters: in five, the omitted letter is *-h-* (*wirling, wizzing*): in four an *-a-* is omitted from the form *-ea-* (*reched, ment, serching, heving*). Sometimes the error is a phonic attempt, as in *ment, relived*; sometimes it is a non-auditory error, as in *sared* (scared) *fligs* (flings) *canged* (changed). Here, the first thing is to check whether they are slips or not: if the writers correct their own errors easily, don't count them as serious miscues.

Diphthongs

In some cases, it seems that the writers' attempts to spell a diphthong sound has caused the trouble. (The diphthongs include what is commonly called the 'name' of most of the vowels when normally pronounced - *a, i, o* and *u*. Others are the sounds in *found, toy, here, air,* and *poor*.)

a	i	o	ow
saling	*brite* *hire* (higher) *iys* (eyes) *sighn* *cryed*	*flouting* *floting* *bloing* *smok*	*grown* (ground)

Considering the four /o/ words, it is clear that there are three different spelling patterns represented:

floating	-oa-
blowing	-ow-
smoke	-o-e

These three forms, plus the *o* of *open*, are the main ways in which the sound /o/ is spelled. In other words, when the pronunciation indicates the sound *o* then it's likely, depending on the position of the sound in the word, to be spelled like this:

Initial sound: *o*	*open*	*obey*	*opal*
Medial sound: *-o-e*	*rope*	*broke*	*alone*
Final sound:*ow*	*grow*	*blow*	*flow*

Another medial spelling is *oa*, but rarer than *o-e*: *boat, coat, float, soap, throat*.

It should be pointed out that this pattern is the same for the most usual spellings for the other vowel and diphthong sounds:

Initial sounds:
a-	apex
e-	eliminate
i-	ivy
o-	open
u-	unit

Medial sounds:
a-e	make
e-e	athlete
ee	feet
i-e	nine
o-e	home
u-e	cube

Final sounds :
(More variation here)
ay	pay
ee	fee
y	fly
ie	pie
ow	low
oe	toe
o	halo
ue	glue
ew	stew

Single-double, double-single

Seven of the eight examples here are single instead of double letters: *beter, faling, tumy, of* (off) *sudenly*. The exception is *breezzy*.

Phonic alternatives

This is the single largest group of words – 37 of the 100 words come into the category. Most of them are reasonable attempts: *nervce* (nervous), *stomack*, *jeles* (jealous); some are less reasonable: *pourshoot* (parachute), *sacond* (second) *nevas* (nervous), *secle* (circle), *trafice* (traffic). Seven words suggest the kinds of misspellings younger children might make (*fritend, herd, crecher, tow, mac, mec* (make)) because they represent spelling in the Phonetic stage (see page 20). Some of these may be slips of the pen, and this, as always, needs to be checked. But *mac* and *mec* in particular, from one boy's work, need attention.

Unclassifiable

geos	goes
ball	bail (Is this the use of the letter name for *a*?)
pourshers	parachuters. (How does she think the word is pronounced? *p + our* is a fairly good attempt at one way of saying it.)

Summary

The analysis suggests the following conclusions.

❏ On the whole the class is competent at spelling. Most of the spellings fall, as we might expect, into Gentry's Phonetic or Transitional stages.

❏ The *type* of error is on the safe side, even though there are some unusual spellings.

❏ The largest single category is that of reasonable phonic alternatives, which suggests that the basic approach is sound

❏ It looks as if 50% of the errors could be cured by a systematic consideration of prefixes and suffixes, or the most common spellings of diphthongs, and encouraging the habit of proof-reading and checking guesses.

*D*ecision-making

To explain and illustrate more fully the process of analysing and classifying, these are some examples decisions about words in the 100-word sample. The six words are:

areplain comeing geos mac, mec rusing trafice

1. *areplain* (aeroplane) There are three miscues: *are* for *aer*; *e* for *o*; and *plain* for *plane*.

Plain is understandable – a simple substitution of a different (and correctly spelled) word.

The unexpectedness of *aer* probably accounts for this miscue: working by analogy, many will use the more familiar *air* rather than the etymologically correct *aer-* (from the classical Greek).

The part to focus on, therefore, is the unstressed syllable and the use of *e* for *o*.

The misspelling may have come about because the writer has not previously seen the word written down, but it is also possible that he has read it without paying much attention to anything more than its general shape and contour: he recognised the word without having to decode it, and has understood it without giving its spelling structure close attention. This is what efficient readers always do in their reading.

Since it is a reasonable phonic alternative, this suggests that the error is one of visualisation. It is probably best classified as a phonic alternative, with the suggestion that any spelling strategy should pay attention to visual memory, and to the significance of the sound of vowels in unstressed syllables (see page 33).

2. *comeing*. The writer knows *come*, has added *-ing*, and has not recognised, or does not know, that the e should disappear. It is best to classify this as a prefix-suffix error: any corrective teaching should focus the learners' attention on the effect of *-ing* on words that end in *-e*.

3. *geos*. The first reaction to this is that the speller needs to be looked at more closely. The inversion of letters and the production of an un-English looking word suggest that the writer may have considerable difficulty with visualisation, and may have difficulty with reading, too. But the right letters are there, even if they are in the wrong order, so it may be that the writer knows how it *ought* to be spelled. See if the writer can proof-read and correct it unaided; classify as 'unclassifiable' at the moment, and identify the writer as someone you need to talk to.

4. *mac, mec* (make). Both of these are in the same script: the difference in the attempt to spell the same word fairly clearly suggests a weak visual memory. But there are other problems: the c/k confusion, and the inability to understand the effect of the *e -* marker. Of the two, the c/k confusion precedes the other in calling for attention. It would be pointless to teach the boy the effect of the e-marker if he is unclear which symbols represent which sounds. So find out if he understands sound-symbol relationships, and delay, for the present, any comment on the e-marker.

The error indicates difficulties one might normally expect with a younger child, or someone having particular problems with spelling. Check also on the writer's reading: he may be having difficulties there too.

5. *rusing* (rushing) There are two possible causes for this slip. The first is a simple omission, a slip of the pen, perhaps because the writer paused in the middle of the word. If this is the case, then she will probably recognise the error quickly if she is asked to read the word. Or it could be that the writer believes that she has adequately represented the sound of *sh* by using the *s*, in which case there may be poor auditory analysis. Classify as an omission and delay judgement about cause.

6. *trafice.* This looks alarming, but there are several possible reasons for the odd spelling. Firstly, the writer may assume that what she has written genuinely approximates to what she wanted to write: the pronunciation in the head, so to speak, gets in the way, so that she did not see what she had written down – young writers in particular tend to assume that what they have written adequately represents the word in their head. Secondly, the visual analogy of *ice* may have attracted the writer, and since words ending in *-ic* are not as common or as familiar as words ending in *-ice*, she may have added the *-e* for completeness. Or thirdly, it may be that she believes this is how the word is spelled. Classify tentatively as a phonic alternative.

LIST OF MISCUES

In the next column are the 100 misspellings collected from the written work of a class of 9-10 year olds during an assignment on parachute jumping.

araplain
areplain
aroplain
ball (bail)
beeneth
beter
bloing
breazing
breezzy
brite (bright)
carged (charged)
cheiring
comeing
coloured
coulerful
creeter
cryed
dangrus
difend
dissapeared
ear (air)
emptyness
erey (eerie)
evreone
faling
fligs (flings)
floting
flouting
fritnd
gentelman
geos (goes)
grouned
grown (ground)
hardle
herd (heard)
heir (hair)
heving
hire (higher)
horrerble
immiedeatly
iys (eyes)
jeles (jealous)
lightley
listning
lonley
mac
mec
medale
ment
nerves (nervous)
nervce (nervous)
nevas (nervous)

of (off)
(opend)
parashot (parachute)
parashout (parachute)
parashoot
pharochute
pourshoot
pourshers (parachuters)
peacefull
peasfull
pesfull
quickley
reched (reached)
recourd
relacxashon
releived
relivd (relieved)
rusing (rushing)
sacond (second)
sared (scared)
saling (sailing)
safly
scarde (scared)
scarded (scared)
scutle
serching
secle (circle)
sighn
slowley
smelt
smok
spleep (sleep)
stomack
strait
strenth
stud (stood)
sudenly
sundenly
sworling (swirling)
terning (turning)
tow (two)
trafice
tryed
tumy
untill
wakeing
wirling
wizzing

4.3 ANALYSIS 2: A PIECE OF WRITING

Michael was 9 when he wrote a piece on the subject of Memory.

Memories
A long time ago when I was six years old me and Neil went out misechifing I chut a stown and it naile it a wondow then we ran off then we came to somedody garben then we clad up there tree and shouted fatet. Then we clad and ran off home then we went back mischifing again we cam to a boy and shoved he down in the grass and piched is sweet and then we ran off then I made a apple bom then I chudet it then we went home.

[Note that 'mischiefing' is an event in some parts of the North of England. Mischief Night in Yorkshire is the night before November 5th, Bonfire Night, when children feel they have the licence to be naughty. Not all adults agree with them.]

Misspellings

mise chifing	mischiefing	*there*	their
chut	chucked	*cam*	came
stown	stone	*piched*	pinched
naile	nearly	*is*	his
it	hit	*mischifing*	mischiefing
wondow	window	*bom*	bomb
somedody	somebody	*chudet*	chucked
garben	garden	*fatet*	fathead
clad	climbed		

Grouping of errors

1. *There* is not a misspelling. It is accurately spelled, but the wrong word; it is a homophone, that is, a word that sounds the same but is spelled differently. English has many examples – *hair-hare; threw-through; doe-dough, to-too-two*. Do not describe this as a misspelling for the purpose of analysis.

2. Transliterations (wrong letters)
somedody   *garben*
Both of these are reversals. It looks as though Michael knows the spelling, but has mixed up *b* and *d*. Although adults and good spellers can also get mixed up with *b, d, p, g*, especially when they are writing quickly, this confusion can be the sign of weak visual memory.

3. Words written as they sound (phonic confusion)
mise chifing   *fatet*   *stown*

There are three different phonic errors represented here.
❏ *mise chifing* is a bold attempt, but the addition of

the -e- suggests that Michael doesn't fully realise the effect of the *e*-marker in such contexts as *i-e* and maybe that he doesn't ever ask himself how the letters he has written down might be pronounced. The vowel *i* for *ie* is very understandable.
❏ *fatet*. Firstly, Michael may never have seen the word written down, and so may be trying to spell a visually unknown word. Secondly, the *d/t* error is caused by the similarity of the sounds (see below), and it may be that Michael has not had this drawn to his attention before. He may, of course, also have some difficulty in distinguishing sounds, but *d* and *t* are so interchangeable that this is not a safe assumption.
❏ *stown* – the diphthong sound of stone (*o-e*) is confused (understandably) with the spelling *thrown, low*. But the miscue shows that the child is able to generalise and implicitly understand rules, and is potentially a good speller.

4. Letters omitted
it   *is*   *bom*   *piched*   *cam*
❏ *it, is* – probably caused by Michael's pronunciation, and by not recognising the relationship between sound and written symbol. He writes an accurate version of what he hears. It is not a serious misspelling.
❏ *bom* (bomb) The so-called 'silent letter' again. He has written the sound down accurately, but has not observed the spelling conventions.
❏ *piched* (pinched) Perhaps he has difficulty hearing the blend *-nch*. Together with *fatet* this may confirm that he has difficulty in distinguishing some sounds, or in knowing how to represent them in writing.
❏ *cam* Another case where the way Michael speaks might affect his phonetic attempt at spelling. But it could also be a simple omission; or it might be another indication that he is not clear about the role of the -e marker.

5. Serious spelling errors
wondow   *mischifing*   *naile*   *chut*   *chudet*   *clad*
❏ *wondow* may be less serious than it seems. His hand may have anticipated the second -o-. If he recognises the word as being wrong, then it isn't serious. If not, it's a bad phonic error. But that would be inconsistent with his other miscues, and it seems likelier to be a slip.
❏ *mischifing* This may have been a slip rather than a misspelling. But the way he misspells the word in different ways suggests a weak visual memory.

❏ *naile* A phonetic attempt based on his own pronunciation, perhaps. But his use of the *-le* ending reinforces the idea that he doesn't fully understand what *-e* does, as his attempts at *cam*, *mise chifing* and *stown* have already hinted. Is he using the letter name for *e*? (*nail + e = nearly?*)

❏ *chut, chudet* for chucked suggest one of two possibilities: he may need help with *-ed*; on both occasions he replaces it with *-t*. Compare also *fatet*. On its own, this is not a serious error. The pronunciation of *-ed* as *-t* is so common that it has produced two separate accepted spellings for several words:

learned	learnt
spelled	spelt
burned	burnt
spilled	spilt

or he may have no real understanding of *-ck*
To use the medial *-d-* in *chucked* indicates again an uncertainty with complex blends.

❏ *clad* is the most serious error. A whole chunk of the sound has been omitted and the vowel is entirely wrong. The medial sound has apparently confused him again, as it did with *pinched, chucked*. But beware: it may be a local children's term for 'climbing trees'; check before judging.

Summary

❏ Michael appears to be well settled in the Phonetic stage. He may have a weak visual memory, and any teaching should aim to help him strengthen that; but he may have difficulty with the auditory side, too.

❏ He has problems with the *e*-marker, and needs to *hear* many of the words he writes pronounced clearly while he is looking at them

❏ He will benefit from having pointed out to him the parts of words that correspond to the various sounds.

❏ He appears to have problems with complex consonantal blends and digraphs (*-nch, -ck*).
On the whole, he shows that he has the potential to spell well, and with some specific teaching should become an effective speller.

What follows is an extended description of the way a teacher might work with Michael.

❏ In marking the piece, draw his attention to the words *is, it, bom, stown* and explain the principles of their spelling.

❏ Point out *wondow, garben* and *somedody* to see if he can correct them himself. Discuss how he tackles spellings while he is writing.

❏ Teach simple prefixes and suffixes: *mis-, -ly*.
❏ Pay attention to handwriting.
❏ Work on the *e*-marker
❏ Give him some practice in listening for complex consonantal blends; for example 'What is the middle sound of *switching, tasted, winter, entrance?*'

WARNING
Recognise that Michael wrote a story worth reading, that he spelled 75 words perfectly correctly, and that of his 14 words half may be reasonably explained as slips of the pen.

4.4 ANALYSIS 3: A SPELLING TEST

I am no advocate of spelling tests. Tests tell you little in themselves, and certainly nothing like as much as reading the free writing of a person. I include this section, nonetheless, because it shows how Lisa, a 9-year-old girl, behaves under stress.

The circumstances were different from a conventional test. The teacher explained to the children that she wanted to get some idea of the kinds of words they found difficult to spell. She would not take in marks or keep records, so they would be asked to continue trying to spell all of the words. Her teacher thought Lisa was a competent speller in her usual writing. I include here fifteen of Lisa's spelling miscues.

loude		throge	through
lowist		entad	entered
whrite	write	coffee	cough
amonet	amount	dhater	daughter
nose	noise	consat	concert
remaine		damestic	
danceing		dutys	
damige	damage		

Where the errors do not immediately show what the correct word is, it's best to write a reminder of the correct word beside it. This always applies when you collect learners' miscues.

Grouping of errors

1. Omissions. There is only one: *nose* for *noise*, which seems worse than it is, because the mis-spelling has produced a rather comic word, and we may feel that Lisa ought to have recognised it as the word it is, rather than the word she meant it to be.

This miscue points to some important problems about testing. Because she is doing what is clearly a test, the words Lisa writes down in this list have no context. She probably would not write in the course of a story 'I heard a funny nose...' without recognising the error herself. But like most children (and adults?) she has an attitude to tests which somehow stops her from checking back for possible errors. Perhaps she even makes more errors in a test than in her own free and continuous writing, because, not having any context for the words, she is unable to check them back for meaning when she reads them.

2. Additional letters.

loude   remaine   danceing

Danceing represents a problem with the suffix. Perhaps she said the two syllables to herself – *dance + ing* – and then wrote them down like that, instead of visualising the complete word. It is a common error, especially at this age and stage, and not serious.

The other two words appear to show an incorrect addition of the e-marker to the ends. Does she think that the diphthong sound of *ou* and *ai* can only be made by adding the -e? Or does she think that the words look better with -e at the end?

3. Reasonable phonic alternatives.

lowist   damige dutys damestic entad consat

In all cases the problem area is in the vowel sound in the unstressed syllable.

❏ *dutys* The plural form of *y* + *s* = *ies* often causes mistakes (cf *fly - flies*; *spy - spies* etc). We have to learn that *y* is a substitute letter for *i* at the end of words, and that it likes to change back to *i* when it can; that is, when there is something after it. It is not a serious miscue.

❏ *lowist consat damige entad damestic* These could sometimes be the result of pronunciation, where a young writer, listening to her own ways of saying words, writes what she hears. But since on this occasion the words were dictated to the child, it is more likely to be Lisa's efforts to repeat the sound to herself and to write down a phonic equivalent. She has substituted something which in each case is accurate in sound but is inaccurate in terms of conventional spelling.

These words show very clearly the difficulty of spelling the unstressed syllable. In all these words the actual sound of the vowel in the unstressed syllable is similar when the word is spoken normally:

low*est*
dam*age*
ent*ered*
conc*ert*
*d*omestic

4. Serious spelling errors

❏ *whrite* *Whr* is not a pattern of English spelling, and there are no English words which begin like this. It is a confusion of *wr-* and *wh-*.

❏ *amonet* (amount). Puzzling. She has not, apparently, related the word she has written to any pronunciation. This may be because by now Lisa is finding the spelling test hard and getting anxious; or it may be because she cannot make an accurate guess at the way new words are pronounced – though this seems unlikely, since she has *heard* the word dictated to her. More likely, she wrote down accurately the beginning, remembered the sounds of the end and linked them together in what seemed to be a plausible sequence. Could she spell *about*? If not, the diphthong might be troubling her. But if she can, a conversation with her about what she was doing here would be really rewarding.

❏ *throge* (through). An indication that Lisa knows what letters ought to be in the word, but can't remember clearly enough how they look. There is also a suggestion here that her analysis of the relationship between letter and sound can be unsuccessful: *-oge* is a highly unusual pattern in English (*gamboge* – is there anything else?) and that should have told her that it was unlikely to be right. On the other hand, since she was trying to spell *through* she may have been putting together half-remembered letters. Again, she is almost certainly not relating what she writes to any pronunciation.

❏ *coffee* (cough). She *may* have misheard the word when it was dictated, but it's much more likely that as she started writing the first string, she almost automatically shifted the word across to one she knows (and can spell! *coffee* causes problems usually). So she's written the first syllable as it sounds (*coff-*) and that appears to have triggered the *-ee*.

Summary

These words are well past the point at which the test would normally stop, so it is possible that Lisa had reached a level of frustration. Feeling that all words were too difficult, she ceased to think carefully about whether what she was writing was likely, and simply put down anything that came to mind.

But, as ever with any kind of analysis, we can still learn. They are not random errors, but grow out of her particular approach to spelling. We might deduce from these miscues that she is at an early stage of Gentry's Phonetic stage, but that she may have a weak visual memory; her attempts to compensate sometimes look haphazard, and she does not, apparently, test her spellings by saying them as they look, but instead assumes that they are pronounced the way the 'real' word is. A teaching programme might well concentrate on an obvious range of strategies, in addition to the Basic Strategy. For example, you might try these:

❏ Strengthen her visual memory, using pronunciation at the same time

❏ Teach suffixes, especially *-ed, -er, -est.*
❏ Give some practice in listening to words, and talking about analogous words and their spelling.

A cautionary note

It would be important to check Lisa's spelling in her ordinary writing. Just as many children score lower on word-recognition reading tests than they ought, because the words have no context of meaning, so she may well be able to spell better than she demonstrates on this test. So you would need to look carefully at her stories and other writing, and see if she makes the same kind of mistake there.

What people are writing, and why they are writing it, always affects their approach to the secretarial skills. Don't ever make a judgement about someone's performance in spelling and punctuation until you have looked at a full range of their writing for different purposes.

PART TWO

Part Two gives readers a context for any work on spelling, and especially about the place of spelling in Language Study. It contains four sections.

Chapter Five: Policies for the classroom, the school and the home

Chapter Six: Myths, rules and exceptions

Chapter Seven: Some stories about spelling

Chapter Eight: General summary

Each chapter is again prefaced with a summary, explaining in more detail what it contains.

Chapter Five

POLICIES FOR SPELLING

This chapter offers four separate statements for teachers and parents, suggesting broad approaches to spelling at school and at home, within the context of the ideas in this book.

5.1 *WHAT IS A POLICY? offers a definition of what a 'policy' is, and stresses its practical nature.*

5.2 *A POLICY FOR THE SCHOOL recommends principles which a whole school can apply to its work on spelling, incorporating it in its general approach to literacy. The section can be used as a handout for discussion.*

5.3 *A POLICY FOR THE CLASSROOM begins from the whole school approach, and then considers how the individual teacher might implement it in her or his own teaching.*

5.4 *A POLICY FOR THE HOME looks at what the parent and the child-learner working together can do out of school.*

5.1   WHAT IS A POLICY?

It is more usual now to hear about "policies" in education than it once was. It is now a legal requirement, for example, for schools in the UK to have a set of policies related to curriculum and various aspects of its organisation.

It is possible that one of the earliest widespread uses of the word in the context of the curriculum was the idea of a "Policy for language", first proposed publicly in *Language, the Learner and the School* (Barnes, Britton and Rosen 1969) and later picked up by the Bullock Committee's report *A Language for Life* in 1975. It is also possible that some of the misunderstandings about the word began there.

Although the word is used freely, it is often used as though (to take the nearest example from the world of politics) an educational policy is a manifesto, which declares a philosophy and an intention, and makes electoral promises. The result of that feeling is that a great many educational policies tend to express a philosophy, and then to propose the ideal world which would be the result of putting those philosophies into practice. Exhortation is an important part of such a policy, and key verbs tend to be "ought ... should ... need to...must".

The problems with that approach are obvious. Exhortation does not necessarily change behaviour, and may, on the contrary, irritate people who don't share the values and may resent being told what they "ought" to do.

It is more helpful to recognise that in the political world, post-election policies are the articulation of the pre-election manifesto. Policies become declarations of *intention*, and describe an expected course of action which everyone who is party to the policy will follow. A policy, then, is the practical guidance to which people refer in order to know how to behave under the relevant circumstances.

The proposed spelling policies that follow are presented as a series of statements which describe what everyone in the school is expected to do when they are dealing with spelling. They are practical, and the principles expressed in this book underpin them. A head or school staff might wish to adopt them as they stand, or to work on them and adapt them to their own special circumstances. But they are about practice, not about ideal but unattainable statements of philosophy.

These policies do not stand on their own, of course. They are, firstly, part of a school's whole approach to curriculum because children write and therefore spell in all subject areas; and also reflect the school's approach to literacy as part of the English curriculum.

The Policy for the Home (see page 74) is also about practice for the parent in their own home. Teachers are expert in how children learn and know how children in general behave; but parents are the world's greatest experts in their own child or children, and know things about them no teacher will ever know. Trust that, and act on it.

5.2   A POLICY FOR THE SCHOOL

❏ **Have a consistent approach to spelling throughout the school.**

That is, whatever you decide applies equally to all teachers.

❏ **Apply it equally to all subjects of the curriculum.**

Whatever the subject, whoever is teaching, the basic principles apply to all. For example, the policy item that follows is one that all teachers will put into action.

❏ **When new words are introduced, spend time talking about their spelling, and their meanings.**

Take it for granted that when you are introducing photosynthesis, or the Eucharist, or Macbeth, you will spend some time in the lessons looking at the words and talking about their spelling.

❏ **Recognise that there are different ways of learning to spell.**

One way of teaching will not work for everyone; the first step in teaching spelling is finding out what works best for this learner.

❏ **Expect learners to take time to learn the spelling of new words, and give them strategies for doing it .**

It will be rare for learners to be able to spell new words immediately. See their various miscues as opportunities to talk about the words and remind learners of their spelling.

❏ **Declare your policy about corrections and strategies in a written statement, available to all pupils and their parents, and easy to understand.**

An example of such a policy statement is given in the Appendix.

❏ **Encourage pupils to have a go for themselves.**

This goes along with a tolerant and supportive approach by the teacher, accepting the attempts, and helping the learners to investigate them. This will be difficult for some teachers, who expect complete accuracy at all times. But for younger children it is essential, and for older ones it can help them to relax and gain confidence in themselves as writers.

❏ **Teach a consistent form of joined-up handwriting.**
Schools for younger children will take this for granted. But older children may not use a joined script, and the school should alert teachers to the issue. Make a decision about who should deal with handwriting – everyone, or someone?

The wrost thing was when I got in troble.
I also like playing on my bike!

This boy (aged 11) can use joined up script, as he demonstrates here; but mostly he prints

---

Consistent handwriting?

❏ **Make a clear public statement that spelling is a secretarial skill not related to how clever a person is.**
The published policy will help here; but you will need to repeat it publicly – in assemblies, on parents' evenings, and so on.

5.3   A POLICY FOR THE CLASSROOM

❏ **Observe the requirements of the whole-school policy.**
Above all, recognise the difference between **authorial** writing skills and **secretarial** writing skills.
Authorial skills involve
  ❏ having ideas, feelings, and information to communicate to a known or unknown reader;
  ❏ knowing how to use writing to think with and reflect;
  ❏ being able to consider the writing and see how it could be changed to improve its effect upon a reader.

  Secretarial skills involve
  ❏ knowing why and when writing needs to be clear and easily read, and the place of punctuation and spelling in that decision;
  ❏ being able to present writing for readers whom one doesn't know;
  ❏ having strategies for learning correct spellings, and for proof-reading.

❏ **Tell your pupils what your own personal style is.**
For instance, will you mark in pencil or something else? on the pupil's own page, or on a separate sheet of paper? and so on.

❏ **Limit any spelling corrections to a few words important for the learner.**

❏ **Teach children to remember words, not to copy them.**

❏ **Teach them to proof read their work carefully.**

❏ **Always show them a way of learning a new word.**

❏ **At all times, talk about words and how they are made up.**
This is especially important with young children, but remains important throughout a learner's educational career, up to and including higher education.

5.4   A POLICY FOR THE HOME

❏ **Be parent, not teacher.**

A parent working with a child should have a completely different approach from a teacher; so don't use the same approaches. Avoid exercises, drills, doing corrections and so on: children already get that in school. Be yourself, and make sure your child wants to work on her or his spelling. Use the approach to counselling outlined on pages 39–41.

❏ **Use the words around you in the home, in the car, out shopping, and so on.**

Children – of all ages – are much more likely to be interested in packets and bottles, newspapers, comics and magazines than in books of spelling exercises. Use the approaches suggested in this book and apply them to the words around you.

❏ **Support the child at all times.**

If you are anxious yourself, you can easily put a child off. Comments from the parent about the importance of getting spellings right, complaints about your son's or daughter's performance, rows about doing the work, and above all critical comments about the child's ability, will all make the learner feel insecure, inadequate and resentful. Feelings like that make it less likely that a learner will ever improve or want to.

Much more helpful are genuine enthusiasms about your child's writing. Publish it. Type it out, word-process it, make books out of it, send it to relatives – enjoy it and celebrate it.

❏ **Make learning fun**

Word games (Junior Scrabble, Kan-U-Go and so on) are more likely to help than drills. Computers, of course, are sure fire, though not all the available games are very helpful – avoid the ones that are too like school text book exercises.

Car games like I-Spy, and the various numberplate games (Make a word from the letters on the numberplate, for instance) will be painless. But be natural about them: play them because everyone wants to, not because you're trying to sneak in some extra-tuition.

❏ **Know when to leave it alone.**

Unless your son or daughter really wants to work on their spelling, don't insist on regular daily doses. As you are enthusing about their writing, and publishing it, you will find the opportunity to talk about the spelling of words and remind them of what they know about words in general.

❏ **Above all, relax.**

The whole of this book is about the proper place of spelling, and the recognition that most children will learn to spell in good time. Anxiety about your child's progress is natural, but doesn't help either of you. Work with them if they wish you to; but remember there's more to education – much more – than spelling, and they may need your help much more with trigonometry, the Council of Trent, or genetics, than they do with how to spell *necessary*.

Chapter Six

MYTHS, RULES AND EXCEPTIONS

This chapter takes a look at some of the common beliefs about spelling.

6.1 MYTHS, RULES AND EXCEPTIONS lists some of those beliefs and discusses them.

6.2 THE MAIN MYTH: SPELLING RULES considers the familiar line about spelling - that by learning rules, one becomes a better speller – and explores it.

6.3 Asks whether there are any RULES THAT WORK?

6.4 EXCEPTIONS TO THE RULE examines that idea, and suggests some ways of dealing with the apparent exceptions.

6.5 Asks whether the idea of SILENT LETTERS? is a helpful one, and recommends an approach to help the learner.

6.1 MYTHS, RULES AND EXCEPTIONS

All of us grow up with beliefs about spelling, and many of them harden into certainties. Their effect on popular opinion is powerful, even though there is often no basis for them. Together they represent a mythology about spelling which can be damaging to learners, parents and teachers.

Myth: Someone who can't spell is unintelligent.

The evidence which shows this myth to be false is obvious. Talk to any educated adult and you will find people in significant public positions who will confess that they are uncertain about their spelling. When I published the first edition of this book, I had a conversation with a senior town planning officer, who told me that he had always been an insecure speller, but that the more important he became, the less it mattered because his (female) secretaries corrected his spelling for him! Among great writers of the past, Shakespeare, Byron and Keats were all less than perfect spellers.

One of Shakespeare's attempts to spell his own name (see also p.83)

Myth: The way to improve at spelling is to read more.

The two processes of reading and spelling are quite different from each other, in fact; and the irony is that the better and more efficient readers are, the less they pay attention to the detail of words and their structure. Indeed, the closer a reader focuses on the spelling of words and how they are made up, the less likely the reader is to understand what the passage is about. In spelling, on the other hand, one must pay close attention to the structure of the word, and knowing the meaning may be no help at all in spelling it. I have known excellent spellers who never read a book, and even more enthusiastic and experienced readers who were quite unable to spell.

Myth: If bad spellers used the dictionary, they would improve.

They probably would, if they knew how to do it. Unfortunately, this confident myth conveniently ignores the problem facing someone who does not know how to spell a word. How would you look up the word "juicy" in a dictionary if you didn't already know how to spell at least some of it? What actually happens if dictionary use is stressed inappropriately is that those who are already insecure with their spelling tend to have their insecurity reinforced by not being fluent and efficient users of a dictionary. As with so many other aids, dictionaries are best for those who are already largely confident with their spelling and enjoy hunting about in them, following leads and making interesting discoveries as they go.

Myth: Teachers ignore spelling, and think it should not be taught.

Of all the myths, this is the most pernicious, and the most obviously untrue and politically motivated. I have been working on spelling with teachers, students, pupils and their parents since 1969, and I have never met any of them who said that spelling did not matter and should not be taught. I have met many hundreds of teachers who were looking for guidance in what to do, and I have met several who felt that teaching spelling, though important, should not be more important than teaching young people a general ability to write effectively. But, regrettably, the truth is much less interesting than the myth and it will undoubtedly survive, even if everyone in the country miraculously became a perfect speller.

6.2 THE MAIN MYTH – SPELLING RULES

This myth deserves a section to itself, because one of the myths of spelling instruction is that there are sets of rules which can be learned, and, once learned, help the learner for ever afterwards.

The most familiar of these rules is:
> *i* before *e* except after *c*.

However, the rule immediately comes hedged round by exceptions, for example trying to account for *height* and *weight*, so it now becomes
> *i* before *e* when it's pronounced *ee*, except after *c*.

(As a piece of autobiographical evidence that rules do not always help, I have to say that despite all my best efforts, I still find it difficult to spell the word *niece* without hesitation.)

Other rules sound like problems in symbolic logic, rather than advice about spelling:
> Monosyllabic words not ending with one consonant preceded by one vowel generally do not double the final consonant. [*Hart's Rules for Compositors and Readers at the University Press, Oxford, 1978*]

which explains why *squeal* becomes *squealing* rather than squealling. Note the word *generally*, which instead of giving one confidence in the universality of the rule depressingly reveals insecurity and uncertainty.

Some rules, attempting to account for spelling transformations, become bewilderingly complex:
> '...monosyllables and words of more than one syllable with the accent on the last syllable, which end in a single consonant preceded by a single vowel, double the final consonant when adding a suffix beginning with a vowel.' [Wheat 1932, quoted by Margaret Peters, 1992]

Now: does that lead you, the reader, to be clear which of these is the correct spelling?
> *benefited*   *benefitted*

Such rules are well beyond the comprehension of those for whom they are supposed to be of most use – inexperienced language users, struggling to find a way of learning to spell; or older, more experienced users who nonetheless have various kinds of problem, real or imagined, with spelling.

In fact, there are two quite different sets of "rules" to be considered, one of which is *prescriptive*, and the other *descriptive*.

❑ The prescriptive rule is an instruction. It presents written statements of principles which are generalisations about invariable spelling patterns, intended to be used by learners in tackling new or difficult words. Advocates of this kind of spelling rule claim that by following these rules as prescribed, spellers will reach the correct answer.

❑ The descriptive set of rules derives from an individual's own thinking about observable pattens and regularities in spelling, with personal 'rules' derived from their own spelling experience, which they draw on, generally without explicit thought but sometimes explicitly, while they are writing.

The first set of rules are essentially folk-linguistic theories about words and their orthography, although in the popular mind they are not descriptions, as linguistics properly is, but *prescriptions*, saying how things ought to be. It is certainly true that there are linguistic explanations which account for why particular words are spelled one way and not another; but it does not therefore follow that the words will always be spelled that way, because the language constantly changes.

Take the word *develop*. It appears to be a simple and clear cut case of a correct spelling of a word, so we can all know that *develope* is incorrect. And yet, *The New Shorter Oxford Dictionary* (1993) merely says that '*develope*' is now rare' and general dictionaries as late as 1960 will show you that *develope* was seen as a perfectly acceptable alternative spelling alongside *develop*. And why not? Think of *envelope*. It appears, then, that the final *-e* is an example of spelling change well within the lifetime of most parents and teachers.

Nor does it follow that people know how to spell because they use those rules. The linguist Kenneth Albrow, after completing a thorough description of the 'English writing system' (ie its spelling) remarks:

> ... most English speakers learn our writing system ... without much systematic analysis of it to guide them. They do not do this by learning each item separately, but by making some sort of analysis themselves. [Albrow, 1972]

For most people, learning rules is not a successful way of learning to spell. Indeed, G.H. Vallins (1965) remarks

> there are no reliable rules, and even the guiding principles, of which there are more than we imagine, are apt sometimes to fail and mislead both ear and eye.

But when learners derive their own rules, either from a study of other people's spelling, or by looking at their own work, then they begin to define the regularities in English spelling – the 'principles' – and become increasingly able to predict how words will be spelled. This kind of rule-making is a powerful aid to learning. Not all learners will recognise what it is they do when they spell; and an important part of spelling teaching is helping learners to make their own learning rules explicit for themselves.

6.3   RULES THAT WORK?

One thing to remember about the idea that English spelling is full of irregularities, is that about 400 or so spellings are, it is true, irregular; but they are largely among the most frequently used words of the language and therefore give the impression that there is a high degree of general irregularity. In fact, research has shown that at least 75% of words are regular, and one study has suggested that only 3% are so unpredictable that they have to be learned by rote (Crystal 1987).

What rules might there be, then, to help learners to cope with spelling? I have already said that the best rules are those that learners themselves derive as generalisations about patterns. Sometimes, they will see the pattern, and not be able to describe it completely; and here, a more experienced adult can be helpful.

What I am suggesting in this section is a handful of *descriptions* rather than formal rules. You will find that the descriptions that learners propose will often be better than these; but these give an outline of the kind of thing that is possible.

❑ *q* is always followed by *u*; and another vowel always follows that.

❑ *i* (pronounced eye) at the end of words is spelled *y* or (less often) *igh*

❑ Words that sound as if they have *o* in them generally spell it with *oa* in the middle of the word and *ow* at the end.

❑ Words that sound as if they have an *a* in them generally spell it *ai* in the middle and *ay* at the end.

❑ English words do not end with *i, ou, u, j or v*. Instead they follow these patterns.

i	=	*ie or y*
ou	=	*ow*
u	=	*ue*

j   =   *-ge* or *-dge*
v   =   *-ve*

(*Spiv* and *shiv* (for detective story enthusiasts) are rare exceptions, and *ski* and *raj* are not English words originally).

❑ The *-er* sound at the end of words is generally spelled *-er*.

❑ When you add *full* to the end of a word, it drops one *l* and becomes *ful*.

These give some idea of what you might do. The commonest kinds of miscue tend to be those involving omissions or insertions involving single or double letters, or some kind of substitution (*-ence* instead of *-ance*, for instance). But when you and your learners have looked together, at the patterns of miscue they produce, then you will be in a better position to work out together your own generalisations and rules. For those who want more help, Catherine Hilton and Margaret Hyder offer several more examples in their sensible book.

6.4   EXCEPTIONS TO THE RULE

All teachers know that as soon as you try and offer a helpful generalisation like "Words never end in *-ley*, only in *-ly*", some bright spark asks, "What about *valley?*" Generalisations about principles are, as we have seen, useful and often essential parts of learning to spell; but there are, apparently, many exceptions to the basic spelling patterns, and it is often these that cause confusion. So:

1. Don't list exceptions as the same time as you discuss particular spellings: acknowledge them but don't make a fuss about them.

2. Where there are exceptions, it's helpful to consider them not as different patterns but as words. As Sloboda (1980) remarks, '... good spellers achieve their results ... by virtue of their memory for the way individual words are spelled.' So the pattern of *valley, alley* (cf. *ally*) should not be stressed, because there are very few words spelled that way.

At other times, the options are less clear cut. The *ea* of *dead* and *head* is less common that the normal *ea* in *eat* or *bead*; but it needs attention because there are important and frequently used words spelled that way. In cases like this, choose for teaching the words most likely to be needed by the learners. Will they really want *treadle* or *dread*? They may: but they will certainly need *bread*, *measure* and *ready*.

3. It is more important to make learners aware that there is a spelling choice to be made, for example between *ea* or *e*. Thus faced with words with a medial *e* sound like:

head	*bed*
thread	*led*
health	*except*

learners ought to be clear that because there is a spelling choice they are encouraged to use the dictionary to check which is the correct form for this context. The same basic policy should be used for all 'exceptions': acknowledge the existence of alternatives, and encourage the habit of checking guesses by referring to the dictionary.

4. There are some words which are simply anomalous, like *women* or *once* or *gaol* (which is anyway being pushed out by the more reasonable *jail*). With anomalies, you either go into the history of the word, (see, for instance, page 81), or advise the learner to memorise it by finding some mnemonic. Most people devise ways of helping them to remember particular words by saying them in special ways. We do tend to remember odd words anyway, because of their oddity.

Finally, an exploration of unconventional patterns can be engrossingly interesting for learners who become interested in the whole question of spelling and its history. For example, using a good etymological dictionary, try looking up the origins and spelling history of words like:

ache
daisy
delight
ghost
guest
health (and *whole*, *hale*)
island
thought
window

Changes in place names are especially interesting, because they show clearly the way in which spelling does not determine pronunciation, but so often limps along behind, fossilising an old or extinct pronunciation.

6.5   SILENT LETTERS?

Adults who have been able to read and spell for years, tend to forget what it was like when they couldn't, unless they have recently learnt a foreign language. They find it hard to understand the problems which young learners or adults with reading or writing difficulties have with some aspects of language. One very important problem is caused by the difference between spoken and written language.

Speech comes first. People could speak English before there was universal public education and literacy, and in the same way children learn to speak long before they learn to read and write. Writing probably originally grew out of an attempt to reproduce speech in a permanent form. Speech is not an attempt to pronounce written sounds.

In normal speech, we do not make all the sounds which are represented by the letters we use when we write words down. We are familiar with this in words like *gnome* or *Wednesday*; but we aren't always conscious that *Saint Paul's* in ordinary talk sounds like *Sn Paulz*, or that *bread and butter* sounds like *breadnbutta*.

In other words, although a lot is said about 'silent letters' in English spelling, they are better seen as attempts originally to symbolise regional or personal differences in pronunciation, or are remnants of pronunciations that no longer exist, as with *knight* (originally the Anglo-Saxon word *cniht*). It's more helpful to see that almost all words have 'silent letters' in a sense. For instance, the sound n can be written today in six different ways in English:

n   nn   kn   gn   mn   pn

A learner has to remember which spelling is appropriate, and it is best to understand that *gn* and *kn* are just as much symbols which represent one sound as are *k* and *d*, rather than that 'the *g* is silent'.

Young children, not being familiar with the way words are spelled, and other, older learners, often write accurate versions of what they hear, which don't match with the conventions of English spelling. They may write *is* for *his*, or *Inglish* for *English*, because that is the way the words sound when people say them.

What they have to learn is:
❑ You don't always say a word the way it's spelled
❑ You don't always spell a word the way you say it.

What teachers have to learn is that a learner who writes *ows* for *house*, and one who writes *ekstra* for *extra* are making the same kind of error, for the same kind of reason. It's not that the first one 'speaks badly'. Be tolerant, therefore, of learners who spell in non-standard ways because the local pronunciation is what it is. You need to help them to learn standard written English, without in any way demeaning their own personal or regional version of spoken English. Say, 'Yes, that is the way it sounds, but we write it like this ...'

Chapter Seven

SOME STORIES ABOUT SPELLING

This section introduces background information about spelling, to illuminate, explain and entertain both teachers and learners.

7.1 *SPELLING IN HISTORY looks at what has happened to our language and its spelling in the last thousand years, and questions some of the more common assumptions about correctness and why we must spell correctly.*

7.2 *THE POLITICS OF SPELLING considers the high profile that spelling has in our society, and what the implications of that are for learners, and for experienced users.*

7.3 *Many people apparently believe that by the time learners are about thirteen, and certainly when they leave school, they ought to be able to spell everything correctly. This section SPELLING IS DEVELOPMENTAL suggests that development continues well beyond that time.*

7.4 *SLIPS OF THE PEN do not necessarily indicate that writers can't spell; and PROOF-READING, either by the writer or another reader, is a valuable activity.*

7.5 *The contentious issue of the DIFFERENCES BETWEEN READING AND SPELLING is discussed, and the dangers of expecting that the teaching and learning of phonics and spelling are the same.*

7.6 *Computers are now familiar in school and home, but little is known yet about the relationship between SPELLING AND COMPUTERS. This section explores new territory, and raises some important issues about what happens when we spell using a keyboard.*

7.1 SPELLING IN HISTORY

A history of English spelling shows us how important it is to be cautious about making extravagant claims about what is correct or incorrect spelling. There seems to be a general assumption that the way words are spelled today is somehow correct, and that deviation from that correct spelling is a lapse which must be corrected: no alternatives are permitted. Most people, for example, assume that *program* is a late arrival in Britain, derived solely from the USA, and associated exclusively with computers. The 'correct' spelling is quite obviously *programme*, isn't it?

And yet an excursion into history shows us that *program* was the original English spelling of the word, and that it was spelled like that until almost the end of the nineteenth century. What about *programme* then? That turns out to be a rather fashionable adoption of the French spelling of the word around the beginning of the nineteenth century. In other words, what we now think of as 'the proper English word', was originally a rather affected use of a foreign spelling. The two spellings co-existed quite happily for most of the century.

And if you are sceptical, and still believe that *programme* is the historically proper English spelling, then consider *anagram*, *diagram*, *epigram*, *monogram* and *telegram* as words in the same family.

Perhaps an exploration of what happened to words and their spellings will help to clear up some of the myths about the permanency of correctness. This section therefore surveys briefly the story of English spelling and points out some of the implications of the story for teachers and learners.

Anglo-Saxon England – pre-1066

Before the Norman Conquest in 1066, the languages spoken in this country were various dialects of what we now call Anglo-Saxon. The basic Anglo-Saxon alphabet of 27 letters, instead of the runic symbols that the Norse peoples used, was based on the Latin alphabet, with the addition of four runic symbols (æ ð Þ ƿ). Depending on where a writer lived in the country, he (it would almost certainly have been a man and probably a monk) would write words in ways that corresponded with the regional pronunciation, so that what was *mann* (man) in one region would be *monn* in another. Sometimes, the variation in pronunciations have come down to us as different words; for example, *scyrte* (an item of clothing) has produced the two modern words *skirt* and *shirt*, representing regional variation in the pronunciation of the original word.

Those who work with young children will recognise in their invented spellings the same ways of representing local and personal sounds of speech that we can see in the writings of Anglo-Saxon scribes.

The French Connection – 1066 and afterwards

After the conquest, the influence of Anglo-Saxon on written language was lessened because the conquerors naturally took control over the mediums of communication. French scribes had to find ways of transcribing non-French sounds. Thus, for example, when they wrote the Anglo-Saxon word Þ*ohte* (thought) the scribes transcribed the runic letter Þ into its phonic equivalent of *th*. Then, faced with the non-French sound *h* (which sounded like the *ch* in *loch*) they tried *gh*, and produced *thoght* which became our *thought*. They introduced other symbols, too, now familiar in our spelling, such as the new use of *qu* for *cw*, so that the pre-conquest *cwen* became *queen*.

The first great influence on English spelling, then, was the intermixing of Anglo-Saxon with Norman French, and the attempts of the scribes to transliterate unfamiliar words and sounds. At the same time, there were other effects, as scribes tried to make texts look clear: if there was a word in which the letters all looked the same, as they did in *wifmann*, because of the many similar up and down strokes, they might change that *i* to an *o*, just to make it easier to read. Hence the puzzling (to us) *women*; usage has preserved the original pronunciation, but has adopted the spelling of Norman scribes.

You can find examples of the runic symbols in this page from an Anglo-Saxon chronicle, relating events that happened between 772–794.

Caxton and Printing – 1480

It is hard for us to comprehend the effect upon the world of the invention of printing. Before printing, the only way of producing a version of a book was for someone to copy it all out by hand. It took a very long time, and was very expensive. It's not surprising that Chaucer's Clerk, living just before printing became widespread, had to choose between being wealthy and having 'twenty books at his bed's head'.

There is a story which shows just how important that idea is. Although we know a great deal about Greek and Roman literature, and indeed the Norse sagas and myths, we know very little about our own Anglo-Saxon literary heritage. The sad story is that after the dissolution of the monasteries, an antiquarian, Sir Robert Cotton (1561–1631), collected Anglo-Saxon manuscripts which had been stored in the libraries of monasteries. His collection was later moved to the Library in Ashburnham House. Unfortunately, this library had a fire, and most of the manuscripts were irretrievably lost, apart from a few fragments. The loss of those manuscripts meant the total loss of whatever was in them. We shall never know how different our literary history would have been if we still possessed those hand-written manuscripts. But until late in the fifteenth century, if a book was destroyed, that was the end of it, unless someone had previously copied it all out.

And then the moveable type was invented, and it became possible to produce multiple, identical copies of a book. Literacy became accessible in ways that had been impossible before. Moreover, the forms of language became fixed for the first time, because the language of books needed to be widely understood throughout England, and because others could now use past books as a reference. Printers had to make decisions about how to spell.

Take, for example, the Anglo-Saxon word *gast* ('spirit' as in 'holy spirit'). By Chaucer's time, it had become *gost*; but Caxton's Dutch or German printers spelt it *ghost*. (The original spelling, by the way, survives in *ghastly*). Some of our strange *gh* words came from the French; but others came from these Dutch and German printers.

The main lesson to learn from all this is that standard spelling is a product of printers, not of writers; and that if printers felt like it, they could impose their own versions of a word on the writer. Sometimes, they simply wanted to make things look better on the page: they might slip in an *-e* at the end of a word to fill up and justify a line of type, or abbreviate a word to make it fit neatly into the line. The effect of printing has been and remains profound.

A page from Caxton's *The Royal Book*. Note the spelling of *ghoost* (ghost).

Invention and independence: 1500–1680

Despite printing, there followed a good period of time when the spoken language was changing, but the written language did not keep pace with it. One record we have of this is English place names. Very often the spelling of a place records a long-dead pronunciation, quite different from how we say it now. For a familiar example, consider *Holborn* (originally *Holeburne*). *Shrewsbury* provides a more complex and significant example. Its spelling was originally *Shrovesbury* and the main authority on English place names remarks that 'the spelling *Shrewsbury* arose on the analogy of words like *shrew*, *shrewd*, which were formerly often pronounced alternatively as *shrow*, *shrowd*'. (Ekwall, *Concise Oxford Dictionary of English Place-names* 1966).

One of the things that happened during this period was that words with sounds which had been present in previous times lost those sounds – like *cniht*, which became *knight* with what we now think of as a 'silent *k*', although originally the *k* had been sounded as well. It was perfectly acceptable for writers and printers to follow their own tastes.

There was a fashion for making it seem as if words were observing a Latin or Greek origin, as in *debt* where the added *b* recalled the Latin *debitum*. Occasionally, they over-elaborated: look up the history of *island* to see an example.

It was clearly a time of invention and idiosyncrasy. Not only that, but within the same piece, readers might find the same word spelled in several different ways: in Shakespeare's time, for instance, one book spells the word *it* in six different ways. Readers might like to speculate on what they might be, before they check at the end of this section.

These variations should not be a surprise to us, but they are. What those writers and printers were recognising was the simple truth that in English one sound can be represented by more than one symbol; and they were also aware of what we appear to have forgotten, that the reader is hardly ever prevented from understanding meaning by a variant spelling. Did it matter to the readers of The Book of Common Prayer in 1549 that they might read of 'thy *onely* begotten sonne' or of 'thy *onelye* begotten sonne'?

One last piece of information about these times: it did not seem particularly important for a person's name to be spelled in the same way, and it often seems as if people either tried out different spellings of their own name (Shakespeare spelled his own name in several different ways, apparently) or as if they really did not mind how it was spelled. Perhaps that is the oddest of all facts for us, because our identity is so closely bound up with our name and we can become very agitated if it is spelled inaccurately. To a Derek or an Ann, there is a world of difference between their name and the alien and despised Derrick and Anne.

*R*ules and order – the eighteenth century

Although throughout history there are examples of those who wished to reform spelling and other aspects of language, the real impetus for doing it came in the eighteenth century. Johnson's dictionary was hugely influential in fixing the spelling, and may have been one of the first widely available dictionaries which people consulted regularly to decide on what the spelling ought to be for a word. Interestingly, although Johnson himself says that he 'laboured to settle the orthography' he adds that what he recommends is still 'controvertible'. Clearly, debate was still possible.

But there were also writers like Lindley Murray, trying to fix uses of language as though they were social decencies. His influence was enormous in making people believe that there were rules of usage which were prescriptive and quite independent of what writers and speakers actually did. Murray invented rules according to his own tastes, rather than making generalisations about what happened in real language. But his book touched a chord in society, and was seen as a kind of touchstone of all that was proper and decent. It seems that in the second half of the eighteenth and most of the nineteenth centuries, people wanted clear, systematic and unarguable rules about life in general, including the English language. The world is more controllable when it appears to work according to predictable and known patterns.

The odd thing is, of course, that even while teachers and others were claiming there were clear rules which fixed the language for ever in a 'correct' form (Don't end sentences with a preposition; don't split infinitives; say "It is I" not "It is me"...) the language continued to change in all its forms, as it still does. George Bernard Shaw's spelling of *show* as *shew* for instance, long after most people stopped doing that, is an indication of both change, and how individuals resist it.

*H*ouse rules – 1850 to the present day

A modern influence on our spelling takes us back to the origins of printing; for printers again influence us through their house-style books. Any publisher, of newspaper or magazine, needs to have an agreed approach, and most have a style sheet which tells writers, sub-editors and typesetters what forms to follow. This is where vexed questions like 'Is it *benefited* or *benefitted*?' are settled. Here, too, matters of fashion are dealt with: *-ize* endings are gradually being replaced by *-ise*, although newspapers and book publishers still disagree sometimes about this and on the whole Americans prefer *-ize*. An interesting question for young people to ask of those whose business is words is, How do you decide what is right? The answers may surprise more than a few.

The final great influence is the newest – word processors and their spell-checkers. But remember: someone has to devise the package, and decide on what the correct spelling ought to be. Spell-checkers are only as infallible as their compilers, and if I personally want to write the word '*headteacher*' then I am unmoved by my spell checker's attempt to make me change it to 'head teacher'. I am a more accurate guide to current spelling than it is.

[The six different ways of spelling *it*, which you will find in Thomas Nash's book 'The Unfortunate Traveller' are:

> *it*
>
> *itt*
>
> *itte*
>
> *yt*
>
> *ytt*
>
> *ytte*]

7.2 THE POLITICS OF SPELLING

The evidence of the history of our language is quite clear: spelling has always changed, like all other aspects of language; and there are conventions and fashions which affect spelling, as they do most other aspects of human behaviour. For the last 250 years at least, spelling has been regarded by many people as a social skill, rather than a linguistic one; and a good speller has throughout that time had high social prestige – or rather, bad spellers have not. A facility with spelling is often regarded as a sign of full literacy and a good education. The truth is that although a good speller is likely to be well educated, it does not follow that a bad speller is not.

At the heart of the political debate about spelling, in any country and any language, is a simple truism:

Spelling is important because people attach importance to it.

When people worry because they think they can't spell, no amount of sympathetic encouragement will prevent them feeling inadequate, because the social impact of what other people think is considerable. Individuals who feel insecure in their spelling often have low self-esteem, which is another reason for teaching effective spelling: it means that people can now join the important club of those who can, rather than being kept outside with those who can't. At the very least, spelling needs to be demystified, so that the learner at least understands enough about how spelling works socially and linguistically not to feel personally responsible for every misspelled word.

Good spelling is held in high esteem, and is therefore seen as a discriminator between people, for example in job selection. It's certainly true, of course, that someone applying for a job should take as much care with the appearance of their application as they would with their own appearance at interview, and for the same reasons: the impression it makes on others. It's also true that the receiver of written communications can be severely affected by how the writing looks. Here for example is a part of a letter typed by a new young typist in the office of a large motor manufacturer, and handed to her manager for signing.

> I have before me a batch of *warenty* claims, running *consecutivly* from 45353-45364 *simulary refering* to *ajustments* carried out to the *breaking* system at the PDI stage ... Upon investigation we found that *vertually* all XX vans were having the rear *breakshoe mechanisum* manually *ajusted* in *adition* to what was stated as 'pre-play' removed from the *hand-break* cables.

The manager was understandably alarmed at the thought of such a letter being posted over his name, and found it hard to understand how anyone old enough to be in employment could be so weak at spelling. And yet, the 17 year old girl had just started with the firm; it was one of the first jobs she had ever done on her own, so consider how nervous she was; it was the first time she had audio-typed from a dictaphone; and, above all, she knew very little about cars. Research has shown that when complex technical passages are dictated, people can become so confused that they misspell words they would normally spell easily. Remember also how Lisa, in the context of a spelling test, spelled so much more insecurely than she did when she was writing freely.

The age of a person affects their perception of correctness, too. For instance: I always write *all right* and am constitutionally incapable of writing *alright*. In fact, tolerant as I am of invented spellings, I can become surprisingly agitated about *alright*. But why? There is no logic in my position. After all, I – and the other *all righters*, – are equally adamant that the correct spelling of other words is–

already	*although*
almost	*altogether*
also	*always*

Change has overtaken me!
But imagine that I was in a public position, and that my words were always carefully scrutinised. Wouldn't I tend to remember the priggish words of Lord Chesterfield in the eighteenth century when he

observed, of the gentleman, that:

. . . one false spelling may fix ridicule upon him for the remainder of his life?

And what would I do if my secretary, or someone who worked with me, used *alright* in something that was going public? Would I be able to sustain my tolerance, or would a linguistic squeamishness, a concern for appearances as I valued them, lead me to change it to *all right?*

Despite all that individuals know about their own shakiness with some words; despite the constant evidence that people of high intelligence and proven ability may not be always secure spellers – despite all this, society still puts the highest premium on the ability to spell. Spelling, like "grammar", symbolises a set of social attitudes, related to standards, propriety and social behaviour. Accurate spelling has come to stand for all that is right and well ordered, and spelling errors are seen as indicators of imperfection, indiscipline, the absence of good order in the classroom and the street, and even (I have had it said to me) the final proof that the abolition of National Service was damaging to the country.

Many people feel deep desire for these "basic" aspects of language to bond society together through universally-agreed norms of linguistic behaviour, observing standards of uniformity, instead of recognising the inevitability of change and development in language. Opinions like these are the more unshakeable for having no evidence other than the conviction of their holders that they are right to believe them.

I doubt if anything will change these views. But whatever you, the reader, or I, the writer, think about them, what remains is the certainty that we have a responsibility to our learners of all ages to give them access to good spelling, and to support them in their difficult journey towards self-confidence in spelling. Ultimately, our message to learners must be this:

> **Spelling is changeable. "Correct" spelling is what everyone agrees, and it changes over time**
> **Spelling says nothing about a person's intellect or character**
> **BUT**
> **Spelling matters, so let's see what we can do to help you be a good speller**

7.3 SPELLING IS DEVELOPMENTAL

Recently, I reread letters that I wrote to my parents while I was a young man at university. I have always thought of myself as a competent speller who had never had any difficulties with spelling, but rereading these letters, I was very surprised to discover that in fact I continued to make some basic errors at the age of 21, even during the final year of my English degree. I consistently wrote *abscence* for *absence,* for example.

That experience led me to re-examine some earlier views about learning to spell. Until then, I believed that spelling was developmental; that up to about the age of seven there could be a good deal of invented spelling; that from 9 –13 most children settle into patterns of increasingly accurate spelling and that if spelling problems continue after the age of 15, the learner needs considerable help. I now think that description is partially true, but leaves out a vital element. Learning to spell is indeed developmental, as Gentry's classification indicates; but it is not developmental in the way that physical development is, where aspects are visibly completed by adolescence. Instead, *like all language abilities*, it continues to develop throughout a person's literate experience. All adults have some words they have difficulties with (mine include *rhythm* and *niece*), and most people feel insecure sometimes about their spelling.

It would be better and more helpful to think of learning spelling as being *experiential*. A writer learns to spell by using words regularly in written contexts in which they need to be correct. Thus nurses who are insecure in spelling will nonetheless learn to spell those complicated medical words they have to write, even if they remain insecure in their general writing. Competence in spelling is developmental in the same way that any other language facility is: people learn to speak in public, to write complex public documents like minutes of meetings or reports, to prepare applications and be interviewed, or to meet strangers courteously every day in the course of their work. All these involve complex language abilities and uses, and develop and improve with practice and usage. So does spelling. Basically, we learn to spell by spelling, just as, in important ways, we learn to write by writing and to read by reading.

For young learners, spelling is one of the many

things they must learn about language use; but they must also learn of its importance in social interaction, and they learn to pay attention to it as they become aware of the needs of those who read their writing. They will move from invented spellings when they are young children, through increasingly confident approximations to conventional spelling, to the time when they have the confidence to check and redraft with growing certainty. Alongside their experimentation and invention, they need a literacy environment that includes a constant experience of correctness, supported by sympathetic intervention and appropriate and timely instruction.

7.4 SLIPS OF THE PEN AND PROOF-READING

'Slips of the pen', and the newer problem of miskeying on computer keyboards, happen more often than we might suppose, and do not indicate carelessness, idleness or ignorance. Such slips are inevitable in writing, especially when the writer is thinking hard, and may be missed when the piece is proof-read, because we expect the words to be correct, and read them as though they were. Someone else reading what we have written will pick them up quickly: it is *always* easier to find the misspellings in what someone else has written. Newspapers and publishers employ people whose job it is to pick out the slips made by writers, typists and typesetters. Readers do not assume that the writer, editor or journalist can't spell if they find a printing error in print. They assume that a *physical* printing or typing error has slipped through, and that the error is, so to speak, manual rather than intellectual.

A teacher has to be conscious of the difference between a spelling error and a slip, just as the learner has to be conscious of the importance of checking spelling when the writing goes public. The *secretarial skills* of checking for accuracy, though less important than the *authorial skills* of composing and imagination, have their own place in producing finished work for other readers than oneself. Proof-reading and self-correction, incidentally, seem to be important stages in the development of writers and spellers, and should be encouraged.

Remember that when people are copying out they always make more mistakes than they normally would; and remember that a proof-reader's corrections are intended as advice to the printer, not as a punishment to the writer.

7.5 DIFFERENCES BETWEEN READING AND SPELLING

It's often felt that reading, or reading aloud, is an effective way of teaching spelling, and children may be advised that to improve their spelling, they should read more. In fact, an excellent reader may have many problems with spelling (so may excellent writers); and reading does not necessarily have any effect on spelling.

Your own observation will confirm this: you will probably be able to read words perfectly well which you cannot easily spell. The reasons are complex, and still debatable, but basically it seems that the more efficient one is as a reader, the less one reads individual words as separate bits, or pays attention to their structure. Meaning is central to reading, and the way words are spelled is subsidiary. Indeed, the closer one focuses attention on words and how they are made up, the less likely one is to understand what the passage is about. The less effective readers are those who read word by word, even letter by letter; and the best are those who are not conscious of reading words at all, but read *meanings*. In spelling, on the other hand, one must pay close attention to the structure of the word: knowing the meaning may be no help in spelling it.

In addition, spelling and phonics are exactly opposite processes. Phonics involves knowing what sounds are associated with letters and letter combinations – a 'sound-symbol' relationship. It is, by definition about reading aloud, making the appropriate noises for particular symbols, or recognising a word that is already in the speaking vocabulary by 'sounding out' the written word. It begins from written or printed symbols, and the reader must know what sounds those printed symbols represent in that environment. If someone cannot read aloud competently, this does not mean he or she cannot read at all: consider the number of us who could, for example, read a foreign language silently and understand some or all of it, but who would find it very difficult to 'sound it out' and read it aloud. (It is also, of course, perfectly possible to read out text in a foreign language accurately without having the slightest idea what it means.)

Spelling, on the other hand, is about symbolising the

sounds of the language into print. Perhaps an illustration will make this clear. Faced with the word *saucer* to read aloud there are only a limited number of ways in which it can be read, given the rules of English orthography. At most, there are between six and ten. But give learners the sound of the word and ask them to write it down, and the possibilities multiply, so that instead of half a dozen there are hundreds of variants. Indeed Margaret Peters actually quotes 250 variant spellings of the word which she has collected from children in the course of her research.

So we have exactly reverse processes:

Phonics:
symbol (i.e. word) ▭▷ choice from ▭▷ sound
possibilities

Spelling:
sound ▭▷ choice from ▭▷ symbol
possibilities

and the problem for the learner is that there are so many more possibilities to choose from in spelling than there are in reading aloud.

This is not to say, of course, that there is no relationship between reading and spelling; but it does seem that teaching phonics may not necessarily have much effect on learning to spell.

7.6   SPELLING AND COMPUTERS

I am sitting at my computer, typing these words, and rarely thinking about their spelling. Sometimes, I type with long pauses, as I think; sometimes, I type very quickly, in order to get down the words I am thinking of.

When I reread that paragraph, I noticed that I made some errors. I typed *somethimes*, and later *wehn*. I can correct these easily. Firstly, I can recognise them and use the edit facilities of the computer to change them rapidly and invisibly. Secondly, even if I miss them, the spell checker on this word processing package will pick them up and correct them for me when I ask it to. And thirdly, after many years of using word processors, it never bothers me at this stage to produce the most alarming and bizarre miscues, because I can put them right, and I know they are generally a product of the speed of typing, and not of my failure or inadequacy. In fact, 'premature editing' – editing as I go rather than

afterwards – can slow me down and make me forget what I wanted to write.

But what was it that produced those misspellings? So far, there has been little research work done into keyboarding, though there is increasing research into the effects of the use of spell-checkers, thesauruses, grammar checkers and word banks. My answers to the question about what produces word-processing misspelling are therefore tentative, but represent a kind of agenda for investigation as the use of keyboards becomes more and more widespread.

Firstly, there is a muscle memory in keyboarding, as there is in handwriting. The work of Margaret Peters and Rosemary Sassoon has made it clear how important it is that children should have a rapid, fluent and comfortable handwriting, and how dependent effective spelling is upon that muscle memory. All experienced typists and users of keyboards who can touch-type know that their fingers generally do the spelling for them, so to speak, and their muscle memory can sometimes be triggered into an automatic spelling of the wrong word. That is probably what happened with *somethimes*: my fingers expected me to be writing something else (like *something?*) and for a second they followed a familiar pattern. Although the result looks like a misspelling, it probably has a different origin from what was in the head of the boy who wrote *whrite* instead of *write*.

Sometimes, however, although I am a rapid touch-typist, I make other kinds of mistakes, which are interestingly related to the medium itself. Word-processing makes editing very easy for me, leaving no visible trace, which means that contemporary keyboarders can power-type at speeds undreamed of by typists in the past, because accuracy is no longer so important: they can type without worrying about the evidence of corrections spoiling the page. The Pitman trained typists of the past would be (and some of them are) horrified at what they see as the inaccurate keying of people today. And one of the effects of this is to produce a casualness about the *sequence* of the fingers. I frequently type *soemtimes*, or even *soemtiemes*, because my fingers become tangled and one keystroke precedes instead of succeeding another. And I can also produce some amazing words because of the sensitivity of a keyboard, and the small size of the keys. My fingers can press two letters easily, and I often find adjacent letters unexpectedly tacked on to words – as in *wqrite* for *write*. But since any problem of spelling, grammar or appearance will be identified for me by the package itself, and can be easily put right, I have a very relaxed attitude to the odd words I produce.

People who can touch-type expect to be able to spell what they see or want to write, and have also built up over the period of their typing a repertoire not just of words remembered in visual or auditory ways but of muscle-remembered words. As they think of the words they wish to write, there is some kind of neural connection between the required word and the finger movements, and the word is produced, generally accurately, without much conscious thought. It is the mechanical version of the apparently instinctive and fluent handwriting which produces accurately formed and correctly spelled words – although that never produces monstrosities such as *cush* for *such*, which I produced just now.

But what about those who cannot touch type? Is the experience of someone trying to find their way round a keyboard at all similar to the experience of the young child beginning to learn muscle control over a writing implement? Probably not: it may be more like learning to play the notes on a piano. We can only speculate, but I suggest that in typing, there is a different kind of muscle-memory in use, which is spatial. The 'hunt and peck' typist searches over the area of the keyboard, and with repeated experience he or she becomes familiar with that piece of space, so to speak. Observation of one-finger-typists using keyboards suggests that this is what happens as they become more familiar with the layout of the keyboard. Their spelling often suffers, though: they omit letters, or choose incorrect ones. For a long time, they tend to think in terms of finding individual letters when they are spelling, instead of groups of letters or whole words as the touch-typist does. The effect of this is make them lose sight of the whole word, and we have seen how important it is to have a firm image of the word as one spells. Eventually, one-finger-typists can become almost as efficient at typing rapidly as the touch-typist; but it seems probable that they use a different strategy to achieve that efficiency.

Concept keyboards for younger learners, or for more mature ones who are disabled, offer some solutions to the problems of spelling, by making it possible for users to produce whole words or strings of words at the touch of one key. And what about the newest technologies, in which "talking word processors" read back what you have written? Early experience appears to show that they improve reading and writing attainment in children. But what effect will they have on their spelling?

The public have mixed feelings about computers and spelling. When pocket calculators became widely available, there was a fear that they would produce generations of children who could not perform the basic operations of number. In the same way, there have been anxieties that spell-checkers would mean that no one had to learn to spell. The truth is, of course, quite different. Spell-checkers don't solve problems: they point out words which are unfamiliar to the dictionary within the spell-checker program, and the better ones suggest alternatives. But the writer still has to make choices, and to make those choices involves secure understanding of spelling patterns as well as the spelling of individual words. Irritatingly, some programs point out spelling 'errors' as you go along, completely disrupting the processes of creation and composition.

What is evident, in all the uses of keyboards and word-processors, is that young writers are freed from the pain, physical difficulty and guilt associated with handwriting, because the words on the screen are always perfectly legible. The very use of word-processors pre-supposes an audience, and provides an authentic context for considering the secretarial aspects of writing. 'How does it look?' and 'Is it right?' become unthreatening questions when learners are using a word-processor, but menacing when a page of handwriting is in question.

What's more, because the words have an impersonal, public and independent existence, and are easily viewed, they do not feel as personal as handwriting. They are therefore much easier to check for accuracy, without feeling any sensitivity or vulnerability, and above all are corrected without leaving any sign behind that they were once incorrectly spelled. Learners become more confident about both writing and spelling - and this can only be good.

To summarise then, these appear to be some of the implications of keyboarding for learning to spell.

❏ The public appearance of words on the screen makes them less personal than handwritten words, so learners feel less personally involved, and so not threatened at the idea of correctness.

❏ Their appearance is an inducement to "get them right".

❏ The whole environment of the computer, including its spell-checker, encourages users to correct and redraft a piece of writing.

❏ When learners are invited to try out spellings, the whole process of testing, reviewing and re-testing is easier and more friendly

❏ As the spellchecker presents alternatives, it demonstrates variations and patterns of spelling.

❏ Because the physical effort of writing is removed, and writers look at the screen often, the visual image is strong, and the writer-reader is constantly reaffirming the appearance of words.

❏ Although there is debate about the teaching of touch-typing, the muscle-memory involved in producing words means that the writer doesn't think about the word, but produces it according to a spatial pattern.

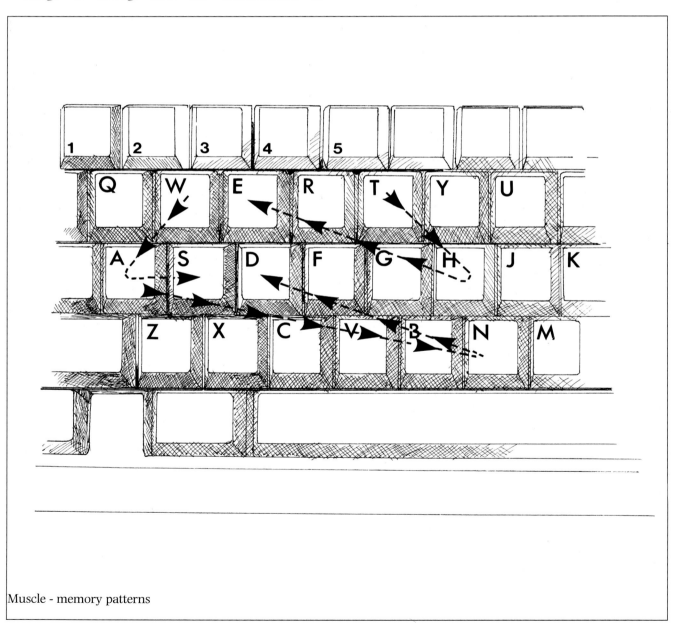

Muscle - memory patterns

Chapter Eight

GENERAL SUMMARY

Put together research on spelling, and the evidence of experienced teachers, and you end up with handy hints like these.

1. Teaching that uses spelling lists, on the basis of studying a list of given words which are then tested, does not help learners to become efficient spellers.

2. Slightly better is to use the list as a test, and follow it with study of the words misspelled; but this causes only a marginal improvement. In any case, the words must be those that learners wish to be able to spell if lists are to be any use at all.

3. Spelling rules are of little help for young learners, because if they are thorough enough to explain a pattern, they are likely to be incomprehensible to the children.

4. For older learners, rules can be helpful, but are best when the learners, with help, work out their own generalisations.

5. Learners who have a good general understanding of sound-symbol relationship, even if they do not spell well at the moment are, as Margaret Peters says, 'well on the way' to becoming good spellers.

6. Teachers who have enthusiasm for and enjoyment in spoken and written language, and a care for it, have pupils who are likely to be good spellers.

7. An interest in words, their meanings, shapes, history and sound, generates improved spelling.

8. The more interested children are in what they write, the more attention they are prepared to give to its appearance, including spelling.

9. When learners in school realise that their writing is for a real public audience, not just the teacher but other people, they are likely to be concerned with their spelling.

10 Good spelling habits are:
    *   The habit of checking guesses by looking the word up, or asking;
    *   The habit of proof-reading (which arises from a concern in the first place to spell well);
    *   The habit of spelling analysis: how is it pronounced? Is the spelling phonetic or not? How can I remember the difficult bits?

11. Spelling is changing all the time, but slowly. What one generation is appalled by, the next generation accepts. Give your time not to outraged attacks on what offends you, but to the more urgent and useful task of teaching learners how to spell, by considering the recurring patterns of English spelling.

Appendix

AN ILLUSTRATIVE SCHOOL POLICY

What follows in the Appendix is a sample of the written statement a school might make for its pupils and parents. Assume that this paper is presented to the parents of young children when they start primary school, and to older pupils at the beginning of their career in the school, with the suggestion that they show it to their parents. It can also be available on open evenings, or included in the school's prospectus.

OUR POLICY FOR SPELLING
A NOTE FOR PUPILS AND PARENTS

We believe that one of our most important jobs is to teach our pupils to read and write. Writing in our school covers **authorial skills** and **secretarial skills**.

Authorial skills involve
❑ having ideas, feelings, and information to communicate to a known or unknown reader;
❑ knowing how to use writing to think with and reflect;
❑ being able to consider the writing and see how it could be changed to improve its effect upon a reader.

Secretarial skills involve
❑ knowing why and when writing needs to be clear and easily read, and the place of punctuation and spelling in that decision;
❑ being able to present writing for readers whom one doesn't know;
❑ having strategies for learning correct spellings, and for proof-reading.

Because we know that everyone is worried about spelling, we have written this to tell you how children's written work will be dealt with in school.

If people have trouble with spelling, it does not mean that they are stupid. Everyone has trouble with some words; and we all have to learn how to spell. But we think that too much concentration on spelling makes it seem more important than the authorial skills, and then it can get in the way.

To the children
We think spelling is important, and this is what we do about it.

1. When you write something, your teacher will do different things with your writing:
❑ Sometimes, the teacher will talk to you about the writing, and discuss what you have written and how they feel about it.
❑ Sometimes, the teacher will mark your spelling errors and point them out to you, and talk to you about what you can do to get them right
❑ Sometimes, the teacher will insist that everything is right and looks good, so that it is easy to read.

Your teacher will explain to you before you write how they plan to deal with it afterwards, so you know what to expect.

Although you might expect that everything you write will be marked and have all the spelling mistakes pointed out, this won't always happen, because we do not think that is the best way to learn to spell properly.

2. Your teacher will help you in a number of ways.
❑ When you meet new words, the teacher will explain them to you, and help you with their spelling.
❑ There are dictionaries in all rooms. Your teacher will show you how to use them, and expect you to use them for yourself.
❑ Your teacher will show you ways in which you can learn to spell words you usually get wrong.

3. If you or your parents think you need more help, tell your teacher, and they will arrange for you to have it.

4. If you or your parents have any questions about spelling and what we do about it, ask us.

Bibliography

Kenneth Albrow, *The English Writing System: notes towards a description*. Schools Council Programme in Linguistics and English Teaching. Longman, 1972.

Crystal, David *The Cambridge Encyclopedia of Language* CUP, 1987

Frith, Uta *Cognitive Processes in Spelling* Academic Press, 1980.

Gentry R. An Analysis of Developmental Spelling in GYNS AT WRK, *The Reading Teacher*, Vol 336 (2)

Gimson A.C. *The Transmission of English* in *The Use of English* ed. Quirk R. Longman, 1970

Hart's Rules for Compositors and Readers at the University Press Oxford. OUP, 38th edition 1978

Hilton, Catherine and Hyder, Margaret *Getting To Grips With Spelling* Letts Education, 1992

Klein, Cynthia and Millar, Robin R. *Unscrambling Spelling*, Hodder and Stoughton 1990

Martin, Nancy *Here, Now and Beyond* Oxford English Source Books, OUP, 1968.

Moorhouse, Catherine *Helping Adults to Spell* Adult Literacy Resource Agency, 1977

Peters, Margaret 'Teacher Variables in Spelling in *Spelling: Task and Learner* Educational Review Occasional Publication 5, 1974

Peters, Margaret *Spelling: Caught or Taught? A New Look* Routledge, 1985

Peters, Margaret *Diagnostic and Remedial Spelling Manual* Macmillan, 1976

Sassoon, Rosemary *Handwriting, a new perspective* Stanley Thornes, 1990

Sloboda, John A. 'Visual Imagery and Individual Differences in Spelling' in Frith, 1980

Stubbs, Michael *Language and Literacy: The Sociolinguistics of Reading and Writing* Routledge Kegan Paul, 1980

Vallins, G.H. *Spelling* Andre Deutsch, 1954

Wijk, A. *Rules of Pronunciation for the English Language.* Language and Language Learning series, OUP, 1966

Index

Index of Names